WILD ORCHIDS OF THE
NORTHEASTERN UNITED STATES

Wild Orchids

OF THE

Northeastern United States

A FIELD AND STUDY GUIDE TO
THE ORCHIDS GROWING WILD
IN NEW ENGLAND, NEW YORK,
AND ADJACENT PENNSYLVANIA
AND NEW JERSEY

PAUL MARTIN BROWN

DRAWINGS BY
STAN FOLSOM

COMSTOCK PUBLISHING ASSOCIATES A DIVISION OF

CORNELL UNIVERSITY PRESS   ITHACA AND LONDON

A Field and Study Guide to the Orchids of New England and New York first published 1993 by Orchis Press. Corrections and minor additions, 1994. *Wild Orchids of the Northeastern United States* first published 1997 by Cornell University Press. First printing, Cornell Paperbacks, 1997.

Printed in the United States of America.
Color plates printed in Hong Kong.

∞The paper in this book meets the minimum requirements of the American National Standard for Information Sciences— Permanence of Paper for Printed Library Materials, ANSI Z39.48-1984.

Library of Congress Cataloging-in-Publication Data
Brown, Paul Martin.
  Wild orchids of the northeastern United States: a field guide / Paul Martin Brown; drawings by Stan Folsom.
    p. cm.
  Rev. ed. of: A field and study guide to the orchids of New England and New York. 1993.
  Includes bibliographical references and index.
  ISBN 0-8014-8341-7 (pbk.: alk. paper)
    1. Orchids—Northeastern States—Identification.   I. Brown, Paul Martin.   Field and study guide to the orchids of New England and New York.   II. Title.
QK495.064B74   1996
584'. 15'0974—DC20   96-34508

Paperback printing 10 9 8 7 6 5 4 3 2 1

TO SUSIE, TOMMY, AND THE LATE BRANDY,

WHO HAVE HUNTED FOR AND SEEN MORE

WILD ORCHIDS THAN ANY OTHER POMERANIANS

IN NORTHEASTERN NORTH AMERICA

CONTENTS

Color photographs of the orchids follow pages 84, 196, and 204.

PREFACE

In the century since Henry Baldwin's *Orchids of New England* (1894) was published, no other work has been devoted solely to the orchids of the Northeast. There are many excellent works with copious color photographs and technical text good for reference after returning from the field, but none is useful as a field guide. This book fills that niche. It grew out of my students' need for an orchid guide to take into the field, and it contains the information necessary to find orchids in the Northeast and identify them on the spot. I hope that this guide will entertain and inform you, and that it will become worn and stained from many hours in the field.

A brief word about the orchid hot spots listed in the guide. I am painfully aware that precise information cannot be casually disseminated, because there still exist collectors who must have a specimen at any cost—to themselves and to the species. This is unfortunate, but a reality. The information given here is general knowledge available in a wide variety of publications. I have simply compiled the dispersed facts and added some personal observations. For those who wish to explore these areas, I wish you good orchid hunting.

Acknowledgments and thank-yous are endless for a work like this, and I cannot begin to include all those who gave assistance and encouragement through the many years of knowledge gathering. Nevertheless, I must highlight the contributions of the late Hazel Bourne of Foxborough, Massachusetts, who first instilled in me the love and appreciation for the native wildlings; "Bobs" Kirkham, for her companionship in the field during my Vermont years; Chuck Sheviak and Paul Catling, for their encouragement, especially during the *Platanthera pallida* project; Roger Bradley, Nancy Webb, Juliet Perkins, Phil Keenan, Shirley Curtis, Sally Puth, Eric Lamont, and Joann and Fred Knapp; and in Aroostook County, Maine, Pearl and the late Martin Rasmussen. These and many others shared and tolerated my enthusiasm during long hours in the field. The field guide would not have become a reality without the drawings by Stan Folsom, who also spent endless hours trekking through wood and bog. To all these people I give special thanks.

I thank the entire staff of Cornell University Press for their support during this project. I am especially grateful to Robb Reavill, former Science Editor, who started the whole process; Peter J. Prescott, Science Editor, for his great interest in the subject; Helene Maddux, Associate Managing Editor, who so patiently went through the editing of the manuscript with me; and Richard Rosenbaum, Senior Designer, who designed the book. I also thank Robert Dirig, Assistant Curator of the L. H. Bailey Hortorium Herbarium at Cornell University, who reviewed the manuscript for Cornell University Press and made several helpful suggestions.

This guide is an extensive revision of my *Field and Study Guide to the Orchids of New England and New York*, published in 1993. Not only is much of the material expanded and updated, but each orchid species is now illustrated by one or more color photos. The inclusion of the color photos would not have been possible without the generous financial contributions of the following individuals:

Ray Abair
Dan and Louise Ahearn
Anonymous
Caroline Arnold
Frances P. Austin
Robert and Maria Barth
Fred and Barbara Boyle
Edgar and Julie Bristol
Gladys Burman
Linda DeCastro
Sylvia Feldman (in memory of David Feldman)
John Gould
Mark and Gingie Halloran
Phyllis O. Hanes

Sturt and Chris Hobbs
Philip E. Keenan
Marion Lill and Mary Lowry
Virginia L. Magee
Mariano Ospina
Juliet C. Perkins
Elizabeth B. Porter
Sally J. Puth
Pam Resor
Sarah Schwaegler
Carl and Jannene Slaughter
Mary M. Walker
Cynthia Walsh
Nancy A. Webb

PAUL MARTIN BROWN
Acton, Maine

WILD ORCHIDS OF THE
NORTHEASTERN UNITED STATES

For well over 250 years the wild orchids of the Northeast have held a certain and, at times, addictive, fascination for botanists, naturalists, and plant enthusiasts. Before widespread development destroyed natural habitats, people thought nothing of transplanting orchids and other interesting wildflowers to their private gardens. Local schools, colleges, and universities often had botanical gardens, and defended the practice of moving the wildlings by saying that the plants would be better cared for in a controlled environment than left to the perils of the wild.

Granted, a few species such as the **yellow lady's-slippers** can be cultivated with relative ease, but for the most part, collected native terrestrial orchids last but a few years under cultivation. Propagation of these plants is difficult at best, and simple division of existing clumps is slow, and success checkered.

Botanists for years felt that the only legitimate documentation for a plant of a given species was to collect the plant, press it, and mount it as a herbarium specimen. Consequently, it is not unusual to find up to a dozen specimens of the smaller species mounted on one sheet. Special expeditions were even held to collect "every last one" for the herbarium.

Times have changed. Virtually all species of northeastern orchids are well documented in herbaria. Diagnostic photographs are now readily accepted as local records for species already known to be established in a state or county. The horticultural public, both private and professional, has finally learned that very few species collected in the wild can be successfully cultivated.

This is not to say that all our native orchids are secure. By no means! Although most colleges now prohibit or discourage orchid collecting, some plants are still taken for private herbaria. And the temptation is still too great for some gardeners who wish to try to grow native orchids. Last, but far from least, development and construction continue to destroy both vital habitat and specific plant colonies. Several organizations now go out and rescue the species that may be moved with reasonable success. But rescue is usually a waste of time; the majority of orchids die when they are moved. Preservation of habitat is the only successful solution to saving native orchids for the future.

We are blessed in New England with several conservation organizations that own many excellent pieces of choice orchid habitat, either purchased specifically for their plant communities or found to have important species after the sites were acquired. Although these properties are not totally secure from theft and vandalism, most conservation organizations take great care to ensure the security of their lands. Laws now protect some species on public and private lands, and more protective legislation can be expected. In certain instances, some states have already successfully prosecuted plant thieves.

Botanists, naturalists, and orchid enthusiasts must take all steps possible to protect native orchids in their habitats. The following rules must become priorities:

Be sensitive to habitats
Take photographs only—no collecting
Carefully document new sites of rarer species
Give your full support to conservation organizations
Report theft or vandalism to the proper authorities

There are multitudes of opportunities for nearly everyone to enjoy, observe, and appreciate native orchids. The following organizations offer educational opportunities and maintain native plant preserves in the Northeast:

Bergen Swamp Preservation Society
Rochester, NY 14602
several excellent preserves in central New York State

Manchester Conservation Trust
Manchester, MA 01915
several properties in Manchester and Essex

Metropolitan District Commission
20 Somerset Street
Boston, MA 02114
maintains several large reservations in Greater Boston and Quabbin Reservoir
   in central Massachusetts

Mohonk Trust
New Paltz, NY 12561
maintains large areas in south-central New York State

New England Wild Flower Society
180 Hemenway Road
Framingham, MA 01701
home of Garden in the Woods
sanctuaries in several states

New Hampshire Society for the Protection of Forests
Concord, NH 03301
many properties throughout New Hampshire

Plymouth County Wildlands Trust
Plymouth, MA 02360
many properties in and about Plymouth County, Massachusetts

Rhode Island Wild Plant Society
12 Sanderson Road
Smithfield, RI 02917
holds many classes and field trips

Sudbury Valley Trustees
Sudbury, MA 01776
many properties in east-central Massachusetts

Trustees of Reservations
572 Essex Street
Beverly, MA 01915
many preserves throughout Massachusetts

Vermont Institute of Natural Science
Woodstock, VT 05091
owns a large preserve in Woodstock and carries on extensive education
    programs

Many cities and towns in Connecticut, Maine, Massachusetts, New Hampshire, New York, Rhode Island, and Vermont now have local conservation commissions that are responsible for significant tracts of land within their towns. In addition many other smaller land trusts and watershed organizations throughout New England have properties under their protection. Each state has an Audubon Society and one or more chapters of the Nature Conservancy. Both organizations work hard to preserve natural areas.

Each state also has a Natural Heritage Program that monitors and documents rare plants within the state. This is the organization that should receive new information on critical orchid populations. The state National Heritage Programs work with the Nature Conservancy to document and register specific lands with rare species.

The Nature Conservancy has offices in each of the seven states, and each state chapter is responsible for the properties within the state and for the extensive educational programs offered.

Connecticut Field Office
55 High Street
Middletown, CT 06457

Maine Field Office
14 Main Street, Suite 401
Brunswick, ME 04011

Massachusetts Field Office
201 Devonshire Street, 5th floor
Boston, MA 02110

New Hampshire Field Office
2^1/$_2$ Beacon Street
Concord, NH 03301

New York Regional Office
1736 Western Avenue
Albany, NY 12203
New York also has six regional chapters.

Rhode Island Field Office
240 Govenor Street
Providence, RI 02906

Vermont Field Office
27 State Street
Montpelier, VT 05602

State Natural Heritage Programs can be contacted at the addresses listed below.

Connecticut Natural Diversity Data Base
165 Capitol Avenue
Hartford, CT 06106

Maine Natural Heritage Program
State Planning Office
Augusta, ME 04333

Massachusetts Natural Heritage and Endangered Species Program
Department of Fisheries and Wildlife
Route 135
Westborough, MA 01581

New Hampshire Natural Heritage Inventory
DRED, P.O. Box 856
Concord, NH 03302

New York Natural Heritage Program
700 Troy-Schenectady Road
Latham, NY 02110

Rhode Island Natural Heritage Program
83 Park Street
Providence, RI 02903

Vermont Natural Heritage Program
Agency of Natural Resources, Center Building
Waterbury, VT 05676

Orchids are everywhere. They can be found within the city limits of Boston, in the median strips of interstate highways, often in your own backyard, and, most certainly, in remote swamps and bogs far from cities, highways, and housing developments. Orchids grow in almost every habitat. You don't need to travel far to find many of our regional species. For example, 26 species can be found within the Route 128–I-95 arc of Greater Boston. If you increase that radius to the I-495 boundary in Massachusetts you can add another 10 species. All within an hour's drive of the city! The same holds true for most areas in New England and New York.

In Connecticut, Maine, Massachusetts, New Hampshire, New York, Rhode Island, and Vermont, 64 species, 7 additional varieties, 45 forms, and 13 named hybrids have been found. All but 3 species are native. Many of the same species occur in the adjoining counties in Pennsylvania and New Jersey, although one of the species found in Pennsylvania and New Jersey, **Small's twayblade**, *Listera smallii*, has not yet been documented for New York or New England.

Although New York holds the regional record, 60 species and 7 varieties, with 56 current species, Vermont is historically the richest New England state, with 50 species and 4 varieties of native orchids listed, and 48 species currently found in the state. Maine comes in a close second with 48 species and 5 varieties, all currently found there. New Hampshire, with 46 species and 4 varieties listed and 45 present, keeps pace with its neighbors.

Southern New England adds an entirely new set of habitats to the boreal mixed hardwood forests found in the north: coastal plain, southern hardwood forests, and a variety of wetlands with distinctly southern affinities. Massachusetts continues the list with 49 species and 7 varieties, with 46 currently found. Connecticut is home to 45 species and 6 varieties, although only 39 are extant. Rhode Island, the smallest state in New England and the one with the least diversity of habitat, still boasts 37 species and 3 varieties, 2 of them historical. These numbers are subject to seasonal adjustments as "lost" species are relocated or discovered and new species are occasionally added to a state's list.

Orchid Hot Spots

Several areas in New England and New York are renowned for their orchids. These "hot spots" are well worth a pilgrimage. If you want to see all the species in bloom, you will need to visit each spot several times.

Greater Boston: The Route 128 Arc

Sweeping in a wide arc around Boston at a distance approximating 10 to 15 miles from the city center, and servicing dozens of communities that lie within 5 to 25 miles of Boston, is Route 128. It commences at Gloucester on Cape Ann in the north and swings around in a broad curve to its terminus in Braintree, south of the city of Boston. In the course of its travels south it takes on the route numbers I-95, I-93, and finally Route 228. Within this great arc and adjacent to it can still be found 26 of the 34 species historically recorded from Greater Boston.

The great variety of habitat within the arc accounts for the diversity and quantity of the orchid species found there. The Metropolitan District Commission (MDC), the Massachusetts Audubon Society, local conservation commissions, and private conservation organizations own numerous properties along Route 128, and many of these habitats will be preserved.

Starting near the southern terminus of Route 128 in Quincy, Randolph, Milton, and Canton, the 8000+ acres of the Blue Hills Reservation (MDC) present a wide array of habitats and species. This, the largest of the MDC properties, includes Great Blue Hill, the extensive Ponkapoag Pond and Bog section in Canton and Randolph, Chickatawbut Hill section in Milton and Quincy, and extensive lowlands near Hyde Park and Mattapan. Numerous wetlands of all types are widespread throughout the reservation, and 22 orchid species have been recorded within or adjacent to the Blue Hills over the years. Nearly all of these can still be found.

Mid to late May starts the season in the Blue Hills with the **pink lady's-slipper**, *Cypripedium acaule*, **large whorled pogonia**, *Isotria verticillata*, and, by Memorial Day in a few of the bogs, **Arethusa**, or **dragon's-mouth**, *Arethusa bulbosa*. Another excellent area is the Stony Brook section in Hyde Park. The bogs at Turtle Pond still harbor **Arethusa**, and by early June the delicate **rose pogonia**, *Pogonia ophioglossoides*, and **grass-pink**, *Calopogon tuberosus*, can be found. **Pink lady's-slipper** and, more rarely, **large whorled pogonia** can also be found in the oak-pine woodlands at Stony Brook.

Cape Ann, at the other end of Route 128, offers many of these same spring-flowering species, but they bloom about a week later. Local conservation lands in many of the towns within and around the region are always good hunting areas. Often the bogs and swamps have boardwalks to make observation easier.

The first two weeks of June are prime times to search for our rarest orchid: the **small whorled pogonia**, *Isotria medeoloides*, a species designated Threatened by the U.S. Fish and Wildlife Service. Forests that are predominantly beech with some maple and/or hemlock on gentle slopes and along seasonal streams seem to be its favored habitat. Essex County is home to one of the several stands in New England. Both areas have suitable habitat for the **southern small** and **large yellow lady's-slippers**, *Cypripedium parviflorum* var. *parviflorum* and *C. parviflorum* var. *pubescens*, but because of overcollecting they are now very rare.

By mid-June early summer has settled in and it is time to search for the **lily-leaved twayblade**, *Liparis liliifolia*, in the Blue Hills. There are several old records from the Hills for this, the largest of our twayblades. Its chocolate-purple flowers blend in with the surrounding forest floor, but the shiny green leaves often stand out. It favors damp hillsides and seasonal streams. In the cooler cedar swamps and bogs the **early coralroot**, *Corallorhiza trifida*, may still be in good condition, and often in these areas and the adjacent red maple swamplands the **large purple fringed orchis**, *Platanthera grandiflora*, is starting to bloom. The **small purple fringed orchis**, *Platanthera psycodes*, may inhabit the same areas, but it blooms four to six weeks later. This span in blooming times plus specific identifying field marks should help you to distinguish the two species, whose color and form are similar.

In years gone by a wonderful area known as Purgatory Swamp in Norwood harbored many of the species already mentioned, including **yellow lady's-slipper** and several species no longer found in this region, **heart-leaved twayblade**, *Listera cordata*, **pad-leaved orchis**, *Platanthera orbiculata*, **Hooker's orchis**, *Platanthera hookeri*, and **showy orchis**, *Galearis spectabilis*, among them. Purgatory Swamp is now a major industrial park, although isolated "islands" of undeveloped land are still worth exploring.

One of the most curious and often interesting habitats is the "borrow pit": a roadside area that has been scraped of its topsoil, leaving sandy or gravelly depressions that often remain seasonally wet. The term can also refer to local sand and gravel excavations. Many of the cities and towns within the region have such areas, and one near Woburn is home to a half dozen species of orchids. **Loesel's twayblade**, *Liparis loeselii*, and **rose pogonia** start their bloom in mid-June, followed by the **little club-spur orchis**, *Platanthera clavellata* var. *clavellata*, and, finally, several species of **ladies'-tresses**, *Spiranthes* spp. These species often occur in large numbers in this habitat.

Wet meadows and swales under power lines are another excellent orchid habitat common in most cities and towns in and around Greater Boston. These areas are kept clear of woody vegetation, so competition is at a minimum. Mid-June to early July finds the **northern tubercled orchis**, *Platanthera flava* var. *herbiola*, **rose pogonia**, **grass-pink**, **large purple** fringed orchis, **Loesel's twayblade**, and **green fringed orchis**, *Platanthera lacera*, in such sites. In early August such areas often play host to the spectacular **white fringed orchis**, *Platanthera blephariglottis* var. *blephariglottis*. A return visit later in the month and even into September might reveal **small purple fringed orchis** and several species of **ladies'-tresses**.

The summer woodlands may lack the array of blooms of springtime, but they still present a few choice gems. The **rattlesnake orchises**, both **downy** and **checkered**, *Goodyera pubescens* and *G. tesselata*, bloom in the summertime forests, and the ubiquitous, non-native **broad-leaved helleborine**, *Epipactis helleborine*, seems to pop up anywhere and everywhere. Careful searching of the richer woods should reveal **spotted coralroot**, *Corallorhiza maculata* var. *maculata*, and, occasionally, **small purple fringed** and **green fringed orchises** in the wooded swamps.

Autumn is a time of fewer species, but some are widely distributed and can be found in large numbers, especially the **ladies'-tresses**. Examine borrow pits, wet meadows, and roadside ditches for **nodding ladies'-tresses**, *Spiranthes cernua*; uplands and drier gravel banks may have **yellow ladies'-tresses**, *S. ochroleuca*; and mowed roadsides and cemeteries are good sites for **slender ladies'-tresses**, *S. lacera* var. *lacera* and *S. lacera* var. *gracilis*. If you were fortunate enough to find **lily-leaved twayblade** in June, it might well be worth a return visit in the fall to look for **autumn coralroot**, *Corallorhiza odontorhiza* var. *odontorhiza*, a small and inconspicuous plant that flowers in mid-September to early October. You have to look hard, for it's only a few inches high and, like the other coralroots, has no green leaves or stems.

Public lands and private preserves that often have good orchid populations include the Blue Hills Reservation in Milton, Canton, Randolph, and Quincy; Stony Brook in Hyde Park; Cutler Park in Needham; Fowl Meadows in Hyde Park, Milton, and Canton; Hale Reservation in Westwood; Prospect Hill in Waltham; Beaver Brook Reservation in Belmont; the Horn Pond area in Winchester and Woburn; Middlesex Fells in Winchester, Woburn, and Stoneham; Silver Hill Bog in Lincoln; Lynnfield Marshes, in Lynnfield; Manchester Woods and Agassiz Rock, in Manchester and Essex; and Dogtown Common in Annisquam. These are among the better-known areas, but many other large and small tracts of public and quasi-public lands are havens to the many species of orchids that grow within the influence of Boston's urban sprawl.

Species List for the Route 128 Area of Greater Boston

Arethusa bulbosa   **dragon's-mouth**
Calopogon tuberosus   **grass-pink**
Coeloglossum viride var. *virescens*   **long-bracted orchis**
Corallorhiza maculata var. *maculata*   **spotted coralroot**

Corallorhiza odontorhiza var. *odontorhiza*   **autumn coralroot**
Corallorhiza trifida   **spring coralroot**
Cypripedium acaule   **pink lady's-slipper, or moccasin flower**
Cypripedium parviflorum var. *parviflorum*   **southern small yellow lady's-slipper**[h]
Cypripedium parviflorum var. *pubescens*   **large yellow lady's-slipper**
Epipactis helleborine   **broad-leaved helleborine**＊
Galearis spectabilis   **showy orchis**[h]
Goodyera pubescens   **downy rattlesnake orchis**
Goodyera tesselata   **checkered rattlesnake orchis**
Isotria medeoloides   **small whorled pogonia**
Isotria verticillata   **large whorled pogonia**
Liparis liliifolia   **lily-leaved twayblade**
Liparis loeselii   **loesel's twayblade, or fen orchis**
Listera cordata   **heart-leaved twayblade**[h]
Malaxis unifolia   **green adder's-mouth**[h]
Platanthera blephariglottis var. *blephariglottis*   **white fringed orchis**
Platanthera ciliaris   **orange (yellow) fringed orchis**[h]
Platanthera clavellata var. *clavellata*   **little club-spur orchis**
Platanthera clavellata var. *ophioglossoides*   **northern club-spur orchis**
Platanthera flava var. *herbiola*   **northern tubercled orchis**
Platanthera grandiflora   **large purple fringed orchis**
Platanthera hookeri   **Hooker's orchis**[h]
Platanthera lacera   **green fringed orchis, or ragged orchis**
Platanthera macrophylla   **Goldie's pad-leaved orchis, or large pad-leaved orchis**
Platanthera orbiculata   **pad-leaved orchis**
Platanthera psycodes   **small purple fringed orchis**
Pogonia ophioglossoides   **rose pogonia**
Spiranthes cernua   **nodding ladies'-tresses**
Spiranthes lacera var. *lacera*   **northern slender ladies'-tresses**
Spiranthes lacera var. *gracilis*   **southern slender ladies'-tresses**
Spiranthes ochroleuca   **yellow ladies'-tresses**
Spiranthes vernalis   **grass-leaved ladies'-tresses**

h = historical record
＊ = introduced species

THE NORTHEAST KINGDOM, VERMONT

This very special area of Vermont starts in St. Johnsbury and goes north-ward to the Canadian border, eastward to the Connecticut River, and west-ward to Vermont Route 100. It has long been haunted by botanists and naturalists for its unusual and rare plants, birds, and minerals, not to mention its beautiful scenery. Many lakes dot the area, but the most spectacular is certainly Lake Willoughby near Westmore. Known at the turn of the century as the Garden of Eden, Willoughby still boasts nearly all the 40 choice orchid species that historically were found there. A Memorial Day weekend spent in the Northeast Kingdom can result in an impressive list of native orchids in bloom.

The rich deciduous woodlands of the region, often bordering on calcareous northern white cedar* swamps, yield clumps of **northern small yellow** and **large yellow lady's-slippers**, *Cypripedium parviflorum* var. *makasin* and *C. parviflorum* var. *pubescens*, and **pink lady's-slipper**, *Cypripedium acaule* (with occasional white-flowered individuals), **showy orchis**, *Galearis spectabilis*, **long bracted green orchis**, *Coeloglossum viride* var. *virescens*, and **Hooker's orchis**, *Platanthera hookeri*. The eagle-eyed may find the rare **ram's-head lady's-slipper**, *Cypripedium arietinum*, on roadside banks or nestled in protected spots in the sugar maple–hemlock woodlands. If you're willing to get your feet wet, you'll find even more species. The choicest of the spring-flowering northern species, the captivating **eastern fairy-slipper**, *Calypso bulbosa* var. *americana*, hides deep in the older cedar swamps and forests of the Peacham, Danville, Craftsbury, and Willoughby areas. Unfortunately, this species is in serious decline throughout its range in New England.

While searching for **Calypso** you are likely to find **heart-leaved twayblade**, *Listera cordata*, **early coralroot**, *Corallorhiza trifida*, **green bog orchis**, *Platanthera huronensis*, **northern green bog orchis**, *P. hyperborea*, **tall white northern bog orchis**, *P. dilatata*, and **blunt-leaved rein orchis**, *P. obtusata*. A well-spent weekend can yield a baker's dozen of orchids in bloom.

In mid to late June the Northern Kingdom is nearly as impressive, but with a whole new array of species in bloom. This time you need to visit the open sphagnum bogs and fens. If you venture into one of the many bogs that dot the region, especially in the Peacham-Danville area, you are apt to find blooming **grass-pink**, *Calopogon tuberosus*, **rose pogonia**, *Pogonia ophioglossoides*, a few scattered **Arethusas**, *Arethusa bulbosa*, and both **green** and **white adder's-mouths**, *Malaxis unifolia* and *M. brachypoda*, although the **green** is equally at home in drier situations. Keep a watchful eye for **Loesel's twayblade**, *Liparis loeselii*, **northern club-spur orchis**, *Platanthera clavellata* var.

---

* The common name "white cedar" can be misleading, because in the Northeast there are two white cedars: northern white cedar, *Thuja occidentalis*, and Atlantic white cedar, *Chamaecyparis thujoides*. And although the two species are similar in appearance, their habitats—and thus the orchid species associated with them—are very different. Northern white cedar, or arborvitae, is usually found on calcareous soils, choice orchid habitat. It is restricted to western and northern New England and northern New York—essentially limestone districts. Atlantic white cedar is a coastal species found from southern Maine and New Hampshire southward. It grows on decidedly acidic soils, which support very few orchid species.

ophioglossoides, both **tall white northern** and **northern green bog orchises**, and, by the Fourth of July, **large purple fringed orchis**, *Platanthera grandiflora*. Without question, however, the reigning monarch of late June in Vermont is the spectacular **showy lady's-slipper**, *Cypripedium reginae*. A wetland species that favors open to lightly wooded areas, it is easily spotted in roadside cattail marshes, at edges of bogs and swamps, and in alder thickets. Many sites are visible from the road and can be located from your car. With a little creative driving and searching almost anyone can find this radiant queen of the northern orchids in late June.

A walk back to the deciduous woodlands offers opportunities to sight such species as **pad-leaved** and **Goldie's pad-leaved orchises**, *Platanthera orbiculata* and *P. macrophylla*, and two of the **rattlesnake orchises**, *Goodyera repens* forma *ophioides* and *G. tesselata*. Although the **rattlesnake orchises** bloom during the summer they are evergreen, and their mottled leaves are noticeable throughout the year. The earliest to bloom in this area is the **lesser**, which is soon followed by the **checkered**. An introduced species, the **broad-leaved helleborine**, *Epipactis helleborine*, is found throughout the region in a variety of habitats such as roadsides, woodlands, and edges of parking lots. A watchful eye may spy the colorful stems of the **spotted coralroot**, both the common variety, *Corallorhiza maculata* var. *maculata*, and the rarer **western** variety, *C. maculata* var. *occidentalis*. Both can be found in several areas. Just west of Route 100, in the towns of Morrisville and Belvedere, are the only sites in New England for the **southern twayblade**, *Listera australis*. This inconspicuous little orchid resembles the more common **heart-leaved twayblade**, *Listera cordata*, and careful checking may turn up additional sites for the former.

A short diversion to mossy, cool streamsides may yield colonies of the **broad-lipped twayblade**, *Listera convallarioides*. And if you're lucky, you'll find a new site for the exceedingly rare **auricled twayblade**, *Listera auriculata*. It looks very much like the broad-lipped, so check carefully. Throughout the summer months wet meadows, streamsides, and roadside ditches are often home to **small purple fringed** and **green fringed orchises**, *Platanthera psycodes* and *P. lacera*. The hybrid between the two, **Andrews' hybrid fringed orchis**, *Platanthera ×andrewsii*, can sometimes be found.

Late August and early September is the time for **ladies'-tresses**, *Spiranthes* spp. Roadside ditches along U.S. Routes 5 and 5A, and Vermont Route 114 yield wonderful colonies of **nodding**, *S. cernua*, and **hooded**, *S. romanzoffiana*, in the wettest areas, and **yellow**, *S. ochroleuca*, and **Case's**, *S. casei*, **ladies'-tresses** on the drier banks. All are easily identified as *Spiranthes*, but time and experience may be needed to sort out the species. Although not orchids, one of the greatest delights of the late summer ditches is the profusion of **grass-of-parnassus**, *Parnassia glauca*, and **Kalm's lobelia**, *Lobelia kalmii*, which grow side by side with the orchids in many roadside wetlands.

Species List for the Northeast Kingdom

Arethusa bulbosa   **dragon's-mouth**
Calopogon tuberosus   **grass-pink**
Calypso bulbosa var. *americana*   **eastern fairy-slipper**
Coeloglossum viride var. *virescens*   **long bracted green orchis**
Corallorhiza maculata var. *maculata*   **spotted coralroot**
Corallorhiza maculata var. *occidentalis*   **western spotted coralroot**
Corallorhiza trifida   **early coralroot**
Cypripedium acaule   **pink lady's-slipper, or moccasin flower**
Cypripedium arietinum   **ram's-head lady's-slipper**
Cypripedium parviflorum var. *makasin*   **northern small yellow lady's-slipper**
Cypripedium parviflorum var. *pubescens*   **large yellow lady's-slipper**
Cypripedium reginae   **showy lady's-slipper**
Epipactis helleborine   **broad-leaved helleborine***
Galearis spectabilis   **showy orchis**
Goodyera repens forma *ophioides*   **lesser rattlesnake orchis**
Goodyera tesselata   **checkered rattlesnake orchis**
Liparis liliifolia   **lily-leaved twayblade**
Liparis loeselii   **Loesel's twayblade, or fen orchis**
Listera auriculata   **auricled twayblade**
Listera australis   **southern twayblade**
Listera convallarioides   **broad-leaved twayblade**
Listera cordata   **heart-leaved twayblade**
Malaxis brachypoda   **white adder's-mouth**
Malaxis unifolia   **green adder's-mouth**
Platanthera clavellata var. *ophioglossoides*   **northern club-spur orchis**
Platanthera dilatata   **tall white northern bog orchis**
Platanthera flava var. *herbiola*   **northern tubercled orchis**
Platanthera grandiflora   **large purple fringed orchis**
Platanthera hookeri   **Hooker's orchis**
Platanthera huronensis   **green bog orchis**
Platanthera hyperborea   **northern green bog orchis**
Platanthera lacera   **green fringed orchis, or ragged orchis**
Platanthera macrophylla   **Goldie's pad-leaved orchis, or large pad-leaved orchis**
Platanthera obtusata   **blunt-leaved rein orchis**
Platanthera orbiculata   **pad-leaved orchis**
Platanthera psycodes   **small purple fringed orchis**
Pogonia ophioglossoides   **rose pogonia**
Spiranthes casei   **Case's ladies'-tresses**
Spiranthes cernua   **nodding ladies'-tresses**
Spiranthes lacera var. *lacera*   **northern slender ladies'-tresses**
Spiranthes lucida   **shining ladies'-tresses**

Spiranthes ochroleuca   **yellow ladies'-tresses**
Spiranthes romanzoffiana   **hooded ladies'-tresses**

* = introduced species

MOUNT TOBY AND THE NOTCH, MASSACHUSETTS

Just east of the Connecticut River and north of Amherst in Massachusetts lies a series of large hills known collectively as Mount Toby. The geologic formations there, including extensive limestone, coupled with the great diversity in habitats have both historically and currently brought forth a wide variety of orchids.

Rising south of Amherst is an area known as The Notch. It is the highest point on Route 116 as it travels south through the Holyoke Range. Several named mountains and hills dot this area, the most notable being Mount Norwottuck, which is just east of The Notch. A mixture of rich mesic forest and rocky woodlands and outcrops covers the hillsides.

Thirty-five species have been recorded from these two areas. The Mount Toby region, with 34 of those species, is by far the richer of the two. The other species has been found only in the vicinity of The Notch, which has a total of 14 species—a respectable number for a small area.

The individual species flower for the same length of time here as they do in northern Vermont, but because they are farther south the number of species in bloom at one time is not as great. As you travel farther north or into higher elevations, the blooming times tend to overlap. Although flowering time covers a longer span here, a well-chosen day can yield several species in prime condition. The third week in May starts off the orchid season with three **lady's-slippers**: the **large yellow**, *Cypripedium parviflorum* var. *pubescens*, the **pink**, *C. acaule*, and the very rare **ram's-head**, *C. arietinum*. **Large yellows** are scattered throughout both areas in the richer deciduous forests typified by mature sugar maples and scattered birches and beeches. **Pink lady's-slippers** are more common in the acidic oak and pine woods. The only current Massachusetts site for **ram's-head lady's-slipper** is on Mount Toby. Historically it was reported from several sites in the region but well documented only in one area, above Roaring Brook Falls. Unfortunately, extensive searches have not revealed it there for some time. The current site is, of necessity, a well-kept secret. It is hoped that as more people search for **ram's-head**, additional sites for this most elusive of our slipper orchids will turn up.

Showy orchis, *Galearis spectabilis*, **long bracted green orchis**, *Coeloglossum viride* var. *virescens*, and **Hooker's orchis**, *Platanthera hookeri*, are often found growing in the company of the **yellow lady's-slippers**. Cooler and damper areas may also host **early coralroot**, *Corallorhiza trifida*. By late

May and early June **southern small yellow lady's-slipper**, *Cypripedium parviflorum* var. *parviflorum*, and **large whorled pogonia**, *Isotria verticillata*, are in flower in The Notch area and on Mount Toby. The **large whorled pogonia** growing at The Notch has nearly 1000 stems. Late May and early June is also the time when the **small whorled pogonia**, *Isotria medeoloides*, should bloom, if we only could find it again. It was found at The Notch in the early 1900s but has not been seen there since, although it does grow in nearby Springfield. **Putty-root**, *Aplectrum hyemale*, was seen up through the 1930s and 1940s, at The Notch, but extensive searches since then have failed to turn up any plants, although the species has recently been reported from Mount Toby.

Before local flooding expanded and covered the bog at Cranberry Pond, north of Toby, **dragon's-mouth**, *Arethusa bulbosa*, **rose pogonia**, *Pogonia ophioglossoides*, and **grass-pink**, *Calopogon tuberosus*, could be found there. The latter two still grow near the pond and in wet, mossy pockets under a few power lines, but **dragon's-mouths** have yet to reappear.

Late June through midsummer brings a succession of blooms. The two **pad-leaved orchises**, *Platanthera macrophylla* and *P. orbiculata*, **spotted coralroot**, *Corallorhiza maculata* var. *maculata*, **broad-leaved helleborine**, *Epipactis helleborine*, both **downy** and **checkered rattlesnake orchises**, *Goodyera pubescens* and *G. tesselata*, **lily-leaved** and **Loesel's twayblades**, *Liparis liliifolia* and *L. loeselii*, **northern tubercled orchis**, *Platanthera flava* var. *herbiola*, **large** and **small purple fringed orchises**, *Platanthera grandiflora* and *P. psycodes*, and **green fringed orchises**, *Platanthera lacera*, all grow throughout the Toby and Notch areas, and with a little background reading on habitat and time of bloom, the intrepid orchid hunter has more than a fair chance of finding them. This is one of the few areas in Massachusetts where the **western spotted coralroot**, *Corallorhiza maculata* var. *occidentalis*, has been documented. Look for it in mid-June to early July. The blooming times of this variety and **spotted coralroot** are usually well separated, but examine the diagnostic characters of the lip to be certain.

Autumn produces few orchids, but Mount Toby and The Notch offer a good selection of **ladies'-tresses**, *Spiranthes* spp., and **autumn coralroot**, *Corallorhiza odontorhiza* var. *odontorhiza*. Both **slender ladies'-tresses**, *Spiranthes lacera* var. *lacera* and *S. lacera* var. *gracilis*, have been recorded in the Toby region in August, and by September the **nodding** and **yellow ladies'-tresses**, *S. cernua* and *S. ochroleuca*, are in bloom. The **autumn coralroot** is an inconspicuous and elusive little orchid that favors rich woods and, at Toby, vernal streambeds. It is in no way spectacular, but it has a very special charm and delicate beauty.

Perhaps the saddest loss at Mount Toby is the extirpation of the **showy lady's-slipper**, *Cypripedium reginae*. The decline and eventual disappearance of this spectacular orchid can be directly attributed to gross overcollecting by the many colleges in the Connecticut Valley for herbarium specimens and for their "botanical" gardens. The Greene Swamp area, where *C. reginae* used to grow, still supports a wide variety of orchids, but careful searches have not yet found any more of this ravished queen.

Species List for Mount Toby and The Notch

Aplectrum hyemale   **putty-root, or Adam and Eve**
Arethusa bulbosa   **dragon's-mouth**
Calopogon tuberosus   **grass-pink**
Coeloglossum viride var. *virescens*   **long bracted green orchis**
Corallorhiza maculata var. *maculata*   **spotted coralroot**
Corallorhiza maculata var. *occidentalis*   **western spotted coralroot**
Corallorhiza odontorhiza var. *odontorhiza*   **autumn coralroot**
Corallorhiza odontorhiza var. *pringlei*   **Pringle's autumn coralroot**
Corallorhiza trifida   **early coralroot**
Cypripedium acaule   **pink lady's-slipper, or moccasin flower**
Cypripedium arietinum   **ram's-head lady's-slipper**
Cypripedium parviflorum var. *parviflorum*   **southern small yellow lady's-slipper**
Cypripedium parviflorum var. *pubescens*   **large yellow lady's-slipper**
Cypripedium reginae   **showy lady's-slipper**
Epipactis helleborine   **broad-leaved helleborine***
Galearis spectabilis   **showy orchis**
Goodyera pubescens   **downy rattlesnake orchis**
Goodyera repens forma *ophioides*   **lesser rattlesnake orchis**
Goodyera tesselata   **checkered rattlesnake orchis**
Isotria medeoloides   **small whorled pogonia**
Isotria verticillata   **large whorled pogonia**
Liparis liliifolia   **lily-leaved twayblade**
Liparis loeselii   **Loesel's twayblade, or fen orchis**
Malaxis unifolia   **green adder's-mouth**
Platanthera blephariglottis var. *blephariglottis*   **white fringed orchis**
Platanthera clavellata var. *clavellata*   **little club-spur orchis**
Platanthera clavellata var. *ophioglossoides*   **northern club-spur orchis**
Platanthera grandiflora   **large purple fringed orchis**
Platanthera hookeri   **Hooker's orchis**
Platanthera huronensis   **green bog orchis**
Platanthera lacera   **green fringed orchis, or ragged orchis**
Platanthera macrophylla   **Goldie's pad-leaved orchis, or large pad-leaved orchis**
Platanthera orbiculata   **pad-leaved orchis**
Platanthera psycodes   **small purple fringed orchis**
Pogonia ophioglossoides   **rose pogonia**

Spiranthes cernua   **nodding ladies'-tresses**
Spiranthes lacera var. *lacera*   **northern slender ladies'-tresses**
Spiranthes lacera var. *gracilis*   **southern slender ladies'-tresses**
Spiranthes ochroleuca   **yellow ladies'-tresses**

* = introduced species

THE SOUTHERN COASTAL PLAIN: CAPE COD AND THE ISLANDS, COASTAL RHODE ISLAND, AND CONNECTICUT

The southern coastal plain follows the coastline from Cape Cod to south-western Connecticut. The habitats here are radically different from all others in New England—primarily sandy pond shores, salt and brackish marshes, and glacial till soils. In the following paragraphs I treat the species that occur within 20 miles of the coast, although some typically coastal species travel up the major rivers considerably farther than that. With a few notable exceptions, most of the species found within this coastal strip are well distributed throughout the entire area.

Late May brings surprising quantities of **pink lady's-slipper**, *Cypripedium acaule*, in the predominant oak-pine woodlands; it is not unusual to find large colonies of several hundred plants. White-flowered forms are scattered here and there. Inland from the immediate coast these woodlands may also have stands of **large whorled pogonia**, *Isotria verticillata*, among the pink slippers.

At this same time in a few scattered sites, **dragon's-mouth**, *Arethusa bulbosa*, is coming into bloom. It favors the sphagnum borders of sandy pond shores, interdunal swales, and quaking bogs. It was formerly more plentiful but has declined greatly since the 1960s. It is said that children sold bunches of them on street corners in Providence at the turn of the century!

By mid to late June **rose pogonia**, *Pogonia ophioglossoides*, and **grass-pink**, *Calopogon tuberosus*, are creating pink swaths along roadsides, in borrow pits, and in the interdunal swales. At the Cape Cod National Seashore in the Provincelands both species, but especially **rose pogonia**, are frequent early summer wildflowers. Also at this time scattered sites along the coast will reveal stands of **northern tubercled orchis**, *Platanthera flava* var. *herbiola*, with its fragrant, greenish yellow flowers. **Large purple fringed orchis**, *Platanthera grandiflora*, is usually in bloom by July first, followed a month later by the **small purple fringed orchis**, *Platanthera psycodes*. This is also the best time to search for the rare **Bayard's adder's-mouth**, *Malaxis bayardii*, along old cart paths and on the edges of the oak-pine woodlands.

Late July and early August is prime orchid time in the southern coastal plain. Within one week you may see five **fringed orchises: southern white**, *Platanthera blephariglottis* var. *conspicua*, **orange**, *P. ciliaris*, **orange crested**,

P. cristata, **green**, *P. lacera*, and **small purple**, *P. psycodes*; four **ladies'-tresses: grass-leaved**, *Spiranthes vernalis*, **northern slender**, *S. lacera* var. *lacera*, **southern slender**, *S. lacera* var. *gracilis*, and **little**, *S. tuberosa*; **crane-fly orchis**, *Tipularia discolor*; **little club-spur orchis**, *Platanthera clavellata* var. *clavellata*; **spotted coralroot**, *Corallorhiza maculata* var. *maculata*; **broad-leaved helleborine**, *Epipactis helleborine*; and **downy rattlesnake orchis**, *Goodyera pubescens*—14 species in a heavily populated and very accessible area. Some are more common than others, of course. The **crane-fly orchis** is currently known only from a few very private properties on Martha's Vineyard. The various *Spiranthes*, which are more common, seem to favor dry, grassy roadsides and cemeteries, and the assorted *Platanthera*s are often found in old cranberry bogs and in wet areas under wet power lines.

The rare **orange fringed orchis**, known only from a few sites in southern Rhode Island and south-central Connecticut, was formerly more abundant and could be found in southeastern Massachusetts as well. In 1987 the **orange crested orchis**, *Platanthera cristata*, was rediscovered in Bristol County, Massachusetts, its only known New England site. Many of the same woodlands that hosted **pink lady's-slipper** in the spring now present **downy rattlesnake orchis**, **broad-leaved helleborine**, and **spotted coralroot**. By autumn there are only a few **ladies'-tresses** left, but the **nodding**, *Spiranthes cernua*, grows in large numbers all through this area in wet areas and brackish marshes. While you are searching for it keep an eye out for the **yellow**, *S. ochroleuca*, on nearby dry gravel banks and uplands.

Pringle's autumn coralroot, *Corallorhiza odontorhiza* var. *pringlei*, is a newly recognized variety documented from Old Lyme, Connecticut. This variety differs from the type in that the flowers are chasmogamous, or fully expanded, rather than cleistogamous, "hidden," or fertilized within the bud, and therefore are considerably showier. An excellent photograph appears in Case's *Orchids of the Western Great Lakes Region*, plate 43B.

Species List for the Southern Coastal Plain

Arethusa bulbosa   **dragon's-mouth**
Calopogon tuberosus   **grass-pink**
Corallorhiza maculata var. *maculata*   **spotted coralroot**
Corallorhiza odontorhiza var. *pringlei*   **Pringle's autumn coralroot**
Cypripedium acaule   **pink lady's-slipper, or moccasin flower**
Epipactis helleborine   **broad-leaved helleborine***
Goodyera pubescens   **downy rattlesnake orchis**
Isotria verticillata   **large whorled pogonia**
Liparis loeselii   **Loesel's twayblade, or fen orchis**
Listera cordata   **heart-leaved twayblade**

Malaxis bayardii   **Bayard's adder's-mouth**
Malaxis unifolia   **green adder's-mouth**
Platanthera blephariglottis var. *conspicua*   **southern white fringed orchis**
Platanthera ciliaris   **orange (yellow) fringed orchis**
Platanthera clavellata var. *clavellata*   **little club-spur orchis**
Platanthera cristata   **orange (yellow) crested orchis**
Platanthera dilatata   **tall white northern bog orchis**
Platanthera flava var. *herbiola*   **northern tubercled orchis**
Platanthera grandiflora   **large purple fringed orchis**
Platanthera lacera   **green fringed orchis, or ragged orchis**
Platanthera orbiculata   **pad-leaved orchis**
Platanthera psycodes   **small purple fringed orchis**
Pogonia ophioglossoides   **rose pogonia**
Spiranthes cernua   **nodding ladies'-tresses**
Spiranthes lacera var. *gracilis*   **southern slender ladies'-tresses**
Spiranthes ochroleuca   **yellow ladies'-tresses**
Spiranthes tuberosa   **little ladies'-tresses**
Spiranthes vernalis   **grass-leaved ladies'-tresses**
Tipularia discolor   **crane-fly orchis**

* = introduced species

Aroostook County, Maine

New England's largest and Maine's northernmost county, Aroostook, holds the record for the most orchid species in a single county in the Northeast. Two species are currently found nowhere else in New England. The large tracts of untouched land combined with the cool northern cedar swamps and endless bogs on calcareous soils make for an orchid paradise. The blooming season is much shorter in Aroostook County than in southern New England, and the two ideal times to visit are late June to early July and mid-August. Within these two periods you could conceivably see all 42 species found in the county. That is, if they all bloomed on schedule and if you could find one of the "lost" species such as the **ram's-head lady's-slipper**, *Cypripedium arietinum*, recorded from Mars Hill.

Southern and eastern Aroostook County is very accessible via I-95, Route 11, U.S. 1, and U.S. 2. In contrast, the northern and western parts of the county have only a few public roads and some private logging roads. In the southern part of the county near Island Falls is Crystal Bog, a 1000+-acre wetland rich in many New England rarities and without question home to the largest stand of **dragon's-mouth**, *Arethusa bulbosa*, in the Northeast. Several thousand plants bloom there in late June. The bog itself is home to many orchids over the entire season. Most of the land is privately owned, but critical parts are owned by the Maine Chapter of the Nature Conservancy. Two fens in Crystal Bog are the only New England sites for the Threatened **eastern prairie fringed orchis**, *Platanthera leucophaea*, which blooms at very erratic intervals. The open fens are often home to **rose pogonia**, *Pogonia ophioglossoides*, **grass-pink**, *Calopogon tuberosus*, **green bog, northern green**, and **tall white northern bog orchises**, *Platanthera hyperborea*, *P. huronensis*, and *P. dilatata*, and, in August, **hooded ladies'-tresses**, *Spiranthes romanzoffiana*. Specific permission should be obtained before visiting areas of the bog protected by the Nature Conservancy.

Spring comes in mid-June, beginning, as it so often does elsewhere, with the **lady's-slippers. Pink** and **large yellow lady's-slippers**, *Cypripedium acaule* and *C. parviflorum* var. *pubescens*, are easy to find; a little later the **northern small yellow lady's-slipper**, *C. parviflorum* var. *makasin*, takes over. At this same time look for clumps of the small **early coralroot**, *Corallorhiza trifida*, in the damp woodlands. **Arethusa** is at its peak in the third week in June, and a late **eastern fairy slipper**, *Calypso bulbosa* var. *americana*, may be found among the dense cedars. Careful searching should turn up a few **Loesel's twayblades**, *Liparis loeselii*. The first two weeks of July bring forth **showy lady's-slipper**, *Cypripedium reginae*, the reigning queen of the bog, often holding court with **grass-pink** and **rose pogonia**. The rich deciduous and evergreen woodlands that surround the bogs feature an array of species, especially in early July. Both **pad-leaved** and **Goldie's pad-leaved orchises**, *Platanthera orbiculata* and *P. macrophylla*, occur in the drier woodlands. Within the cedar and alder groves and thickets grow several of the **twayblades: broad-lipped**, *Listera convallarioides*, **auricled**, *L. auriculata*, and **heart-leaved**, *L. cordata*. **Green adder's-mouth**, *Malaxis unifolia*, can be found in both moist and drier areas. A watchful eye may detect a few plants of the rare **white adder's-mouth**, *Malaxis brachypoda*, hidden in the sphagnum moss among the cedars and alders. **Large** and **small purple fringed orchises**, *Platanthera grandiflora* and *P. psycodes*, dot the open streamsides and less dense wooded wetlands, and **spotted coralroot**, *Corallorhiza maculata* var. *maculata*, pops up here and there in the woodlands, often in the same areas where the less common **western spotted coralroot**, *C. maculata* var. *occidentalis*, was blooming several weeks earlier.

Northward toward Caribou is the valley of the Aroostook River, where in early July scattered clumps of **northern tubercled orchis**, *Platanthera flava* var. *herbiola*, and **shining ladies'-tresses**, *Spiranthes lucida*, may be found. The broad, grassy cobbles along the river often have **large purple fringed orchis** standing up to 80 cm tall among the vegetation.

If you visit Caribou a bit earlier, in late June, the enchanting **small round-leaved orchis**, *Amerorchis rotundifolia*, is in bloom. Currently, this is the only area in the Northeast where you can readily see this species. There are several excellent orchid sites about Caribou, all in private holdings, including Nature

Conservancy properties. **Large yellow lady's-slipper** is frequent to locally abundant in the Caribou area and often can be seen from the roadsides; one site has in excess of 3000 flowering plants. Scattered in second-growth deciduous woodlands are the fantastic gargoyle-like flowers of **Hooker's orchis**, *Platanthera hookeri*.

Borrow pits and power line wetlands often provide habitat for **Loesel's twayblade, northern club-spur orchis**, *Platanthera clavellata* var. *ophioglossoides*, **tall white northern** and **green bog orchises**, and, later in the season, both **hooded** and **nodding ladies'-tresses**, *Spiranthes cernua*. Look for **northern slender** and **yellow ladies'-tresses**, *Spiranthes lacera* var. *lacera* and *S. ochroleuca*, on drier banks and in oldfields. A single historical report of **Case's ladies'-tresses**, *S. casei*, came from near Houlton, Maine, in 1965. This species may occur in Aroostook County, as its habitat abounds there, but it is currently known in Maine only from near Rangely, in Franklin County, and from northern Oxford Country, where it was discovered in 1996. It blooms around the first of September.

Following U.S. 1 north to its beginning in Fort Kent and then west to Allagash will take you to some of the most remote but still accessible botanical areas in New England. Long famed as the home of the **Furbish lousewort**, *Pedicularis furbishiae*, an Endangered member of the figwort family, the banks, bogs, and swales of the St. John River valley feature some of the same orchids that grow elsewhere in the county. Northern Aroostook's specialty is the **giant rattlesnake orchis**, *Goodyera oblongifolia*. Although historically found in other sites in Aroostook County, the only site currently known is near Fort Kent. Diligent searching of the deciduous woodlands may reveal more. An enormous stand of nearly 1000 plants found in 1981 at Bald Mountain, near Ashland, has since been destroyed by logging and mining interests.

Aroostook County is a long way from almost anywhere else in New England, but a journey there in either late June and early July or mid-August is certain to be rewarding.

Species List for Aroostook County

Amerorchis rotundifolia   **small round-leaved orchis**
Arethusa bulbosa   **dragon's-mouth**
Calopogon tuberosus   **grass-pink**
Calypso bulbosa var. *americana*   **eastern fairy-slipper**
Coeloglossum viride var. *virescens*   **long bracted green orchis**
Corallorhiza maculata var. *maculata*   **spotted coralroot**
Corallorhiza maculata var. *occidentalis*   **western spotted coralroot**
Corallorhiza trifida   **early coralroot**
Cypripedium acaule   **pink lady's-slipper, or moccasin flower**
Cypripedium arietinum   **ram's-head lady's-slipper**

Cypripedium parviflorum var. *makasin*   **northern small yellow lady's-slipper**
Cypripedium parviflorum var. *pubescens*   **large yellow lady's-slipper**
Cypripedium reginae   **showy lady's-slipper**
Epipactis helleborine   **broad-leaved helleborine***
Goodyera oblongifolia   **giant rattlesnake orchis**
Goodyera repens forma *ophioides*   **lesser rattlesnake orchis**
Goodyera tesselata   **checkered rattlesnake orchis**
Liparis loeselii   **Loesel's twayblade, or fen orchis**
Listera convallarioides   **broad-lipped twayblade**
Listera cordata   **heart-leaved twayblade**
Malaxis brachypoda   **white adder's-mouth**
Malaxis unifolia   **green adder's-mouth**
Platanthera blephariglottis var. *blephariglottis*   **northern white fringed orchis**
Platanthera clavellata var. *ophioglossoides*   **northern club-spur orchis**
Platanthera dilatata   **tall white northern bog orchis**
Platanthera flava var. *herbiola*   **northern tubercled orchis**
Platanthera grandiflora   **large purple fringed orchis**
Platanthera hookeri   **Hooker's orchis**
Platanthera huronensis   **green bog orchis**
Platanthera hyperborea   **northern green bog orchis**
Platanthera lacera   **green fringed orchis, or ragged orchis**
Platanthera leucophaea   **eastern prairie fringed orchis**
Platanthera macrophylla   **Goldie's pad-leaved orchis, or large pad-leaved orchis**
Platanthera obtusata   **blunt-leaved rein orchis**
Platanthera orbiculata   **pad-leaved orchis**
Platanthera psycodes   **small purple fringed orchis**
Pogonia ophioglossoides   **rose pogonia**
Spiranthes cernua   **nodding ladies'-tresses**
Spiranthes lacera var. *lacera*   **northern slender ladies'-tresses**
Spiranthes lucida   **shining ladies'-tresses**
Spiranthes ochroleuca   **yellow ladies'-tresses**
Spiranthes romanzoffiana   **hooded ladies'-tresses**

* = introduced species

CENTRAL NEW YORK STATE: ROCHESTER AND SYRACUSE

Spring in central New York is an orchidist's paradise. Within a few hours' drive it is possible to see more than a dozen species in bloom, two of which cannot be seen elsewhere in the Northeast.

Mid to late May is an ideal time to visit the Rochester area. Begin at the fabled Bergen Swamp on the west side of the city. Although it is not the only site in New York for **small white lady's-slipper**, *Cypripedium candidum*,

Bergen Swamp is certainly the best known. It and several other important properties are owned by the Bergen Swamp Preservation Society, a private conservation organization whose efforts have resulted in the preservation of large tracts of valuable natural areas. A visit to the fen at Bergen Swamp reveals not only many clumps of **small white lady's-slipper**, but also **northern small yellow** and **large yellow lady's-slipper**, *Cypripedium parviflorum* var. *makasin* and *C. parviflorum* var. *pubescens*, and their hybrids, **Andrews' hybrid lady's-slipper**, *C.* ✕*andrewsii*, and **Faville's hybrid lady's-slipper**, *C.* ✕*andrewsii* nm. *favillianum*. On your way to the fen watch for **pink lady's-slipper**, *Cypripedium acaule*, **early coralroot**, *Corallorhiza trifida*, and **long bracted green orchis**, *Coeloglossum viride* var. *virescens*, in the surrounding woodlands, and perhaps a massasauga rattlesnake. The snakes are quite rare and very shy, so don't plan your trip around them.

After feasting on the various **lady's-slippers** at Bergen, take a short drive to the east side of Rochester to the town of Zurich and another Bergen Swamp Preservation Society property, Zurich Bog. The large quaking bog, swamp, and extensive rich woodland offer quantities of **large yellow lady's-slippers**, scattered **northern small yellow lady's-slippers**, and, later in June, **showy lady's-slipper**, *Cypripedium reginae*. The very observant may find a few colonies of the elusive **southern twayblade**, *Listera australis*. Both **early coralroot** and **western spotted coralroot**, *Corallorhiza maculata* var. *occidentalis*, can be found in season; and, of course, **pink lady's-slippers** and the various **rattlesnake orchises**, *Goodyera* spp., are ever present.

Later in the season, in July, **long bracted green orchis** and **northern club-spur orchis**, *Platanthera clavellata* var. *ophioglossoides*, bloom. Search marshy wet meadows, power lines, and open wooded swamps for **fringed orchises: green**, *Platanthera lacera*, **small purple**, *P. psycodes*, and **white**, *P. blephariglottis* var. *blephariglottis*. Historically the reclusive **eastern prairie fringed orchis**, *P. leucophaea*, was found in this area, but it has been many years since it was last seen.

The Syracuse area offers many of the same woodland species as Rochester; in addition, the only current site in New York State for the **striped coralroot**, *Corallorhiza striata*, and an excellent stand of **ram's-head lady's-slipper**, *Cypripedium arietinum*, are just east of Syracuse. This area also supports all the other **lady's-slippers** with the exception of the **small white**, which historically was found within the edge of the city of Syracuse.

An excellent place to search for many of the familiar species is Clark Reservation in Jamesville. The extensive limestone woodlands and outcrops are famous for ferns, notably the **American hart's-tongue**, *Phyllitis scolopendrium* var. *americanum*, but should be equally famous for orchids. **Hooker's orchis**, *Platanthera hookeri*, and **Goldie's pad-leaved** and **pad-leaved orchises**, *Platanthera macrophylla* and *P. orbiculata*, grow within these woodlands. **Small whorled pogonia**, *Isotria medeoloides*, has been reported from this area, and **autumn coralroot**, *Corallorhiza odontorhiza* var. *odontorhiza*, can be abundant.

By autumn, fen and bog and roadside ditches are resplendent with a variety of **ladies'-tresses**, *Spiranthes* spp. Starting in late July to mid-August watch for **northern slender** and **southern slender ladies'-tresses**, *Spiranthes lacera* var. *lacera* and *S. lacera* var. *gracilis*, on roadside banks, cemeteries, and oldfields. August brings **hooded ladies'-tresses**, *S. romanzoffiana*, in the northern calcareous wetlands, followed by the polymorphic **nodding ladies'-tresses**, *S. cernua*, which often are accompanied in the drier areas by **yellow ladies'-tresses**, *S. ochroleuca*. Look carefully and you may spy **autumn coralroot** in the rich woodlands in late September into early October.

Several species were historically found in the Rochester-Syracuse area. **Eastern prairie fringed orchis**, **small round-leaved orchis**, *Amerorchis rotundifolia*, **eastern fairy-slipper**, *Calypso bulbosa* var. *americana*, and **orange fringed orchis**, *Platanthera ciliaris*, have all been recorded from the region. Although the landscape has changed greatly, there is still abundant suitable habitat for these species, and some or all may yet be found again.

Species List for Central New York

Amerorchis rotundifolia   **small round-leaved orchis**[h]
Arethusa bulbosa   **dragon's-mouth**
Calopogon tuberosus   **grass-pink**
Calypso bulbosa var. *americana*   **eastern fairy-slipper**[h]
Coeloglossum viride var. *virescens*   **long bracted green orchis**
Corallorhiza maculata var. *maculata*   **spotted coralroot**
Corallorhiza maculata var. *occidentalis*   **western spotted coralroot**
Corallorhiza odontorhiza var. *odontorhiza*   **autumn coralroot**
Corallorhiza striata   **striped coralroot**
Corallorhiza trifida   **early coralroot**
Cypripedium acaule   **pink lady's-slipper, or moccasin flower**
Cypripedium arietinum   **ram's-head lady's-slipper**
Cypripedium candidum   **small white lady's-slipper**
Cypripedium parviflorum var. *makasin*   **northern small yellow lady's-slipper**
Cypripedium parviflorum var. *pubescens*   **large yellow lady's-slipper**
Cypripedium reginae   **showy lady's-slipper**
Epipactis helleborine   **broad-leaved helleborine***
Galearis spectabilis   **showy orchis**
Goodyera pubescens   **downy rattlesnake orchis**
Goodyera tesselata   **checkered rattlesnake orchis**
Isotria medeoloides   **small whorled pogonia**
Liparis loeselii   **Loesel's twayblade, or fen orchis**

Listera australis   **southern twayblade**
Listera cordata   **heart-leaved twayblade**
Malaxis brachypoda   **white adder's-mouth**
Malaxis unifolia   **green adder's-mouth**
Platanthera blephariglottis var. *blephariglottis*   **white fringed orchis**
Platanthera ciliaris   **orange (yellow) fringed orchis**[h]
Platanthera clavellata var. *ophioglossoides*   **northern club-spur orchis**
Platanthera dilatata   **tall white northern bog orchis**
Platanthera grandiflora   **large purple fringed orchis**
Platanthera hookeri   **Hooker's orchis**
Platanthera huronensis   **green bog orchis**
Platanthera hyperborea   **northern green bog orchis**
Platanthera lacera   **green fringed orchis, or ragged orchis**
Platanthera leucophaea   **eastern prairie fringed orchis**[h]
Platanthera macrophylla   **Goldie's pad-leaved orchis, or large pad-leaved orchis**
Platanthera orbiculata   **pad-leaved orchis**
Platanthera psycodes   **small purple fringed orchis**
Pogonia ophioglossoides   **rose pogonia**
Spiranthes cernua   **nodding ladies'-tresses**
Spiranthes lacera var. *lacera*   **northern slender ladies'-tresses**
Spiranthes lacera var. *gracilis*   **southern slender ladies'-tresses**
Spiranthes lucida   **shining ladies'-tresses**
Spiranthes ochroleuca   **yellow ladies'-tresses**
Spiranthes romanzoffiana   **hooded ladies'-tresses**

h = historical record
* = introduced species

Eastern Long Island

Although Long Island is very heavily populated, the eastern end still features an exciting array of orchids, including one endemic species and some that are not easily seen elsewhere in the Northeast.

Spring is familiar with quantities of **pink lady's-slipper**, *Cypripedium acaule*, and an occasional **large whorled pogonia**, *Isotria verticillata*. But this area, like the southern coastal plain of New England, comes into its glory in midsummer. A single visit to the north and south forks of eastern Long Island in early August can be one of the most rewarding orchid forays of the year.

Begin in the Greenport area, where mixed beech woodlands offer the **crane-fly orchis**, *Tipularia discolor*, near the northern limit of its range and an occasional **spotted coralroot**, *Corallorhiza maculata* var. *maculata*. Continuing on with two short ferry rides to the south fork, watch roadside berms and ditches for **southern white fringed orchis**, *Platanthera blephariglottis* var. *conspicua*, **orange crested orchis**, *P. cristata*, **orange fringed orchis**, *P. ciliaris*, and their various hybrids: **bicolor hybrid fringed orchis**, *P. ×bicolor*, **Canby's hybrid fringed orchis**, *P. ×canbyi*, and **Channell's hybrid fringed orchis**, *P. ×channellii*, along with **little club-spur orchis**, *P. clavellata* var. *clavellata*. The rare **Bayard's adder's-mouth**, *Malaxis bayardii*, occurs (and has occurred historically) in a few of the drier roadside banks, dune hollows, and cemeteries. In the past **Bayard's adder's-mouth** has been confused with **green-adder's mouth**, *Malaxis unifolia*. Some old records for **green-adder's mouth** from xeric sites may actually be for **Bayard's adder's-mouth**. You can ascertain the accuracy of the identification by comparing the field marks given in the record with those listed on p. 123 for the two species.

In the dry interdunal hollows of the Montauk region grows the **pale fringed orchis**, *Platanthera pallida*, New York's only endemic orchid. Its recent taxonomic description was one of the most exciting botanical events in many years in the Northeast. The plants tend to occur in fair numbers in dry interdunal hollows under mature pitch pine. Also watch for **southern slender ladies'-tresses**, *Spiranthes lacera* var. *gracilis*, which grows in similar habitats. Earlier in the season, in late June and early July, some of the wet interdunal swales are painted shades of pink with **rose pogonia**, *Pogonia ophioglossoides*, and **grass-pink**, *Calopogon tuberosus*. Hither Hills State Park is a particularly good spot for these two species.

One of the more recent records for New York and the Northeast is **giant ladies'-tresses**, *Spiranthes praecox*. The late Joe Beitel found a small colony in a swampy wood in Montauk near one of the bordering ponds in the late 1980s. Typical *S. praecox* from the southern states blooms in late spring, and the flowers usually have prominent raised green veins in the lip. Occasional records of plants lacking this green coloring have been noted. The *S. praecox* from Delaware and New Jersey is a fall-blooming swampland species with entirely white lips. At this time the New York plants appear to be identical with those in New Jersey in both morphology and blooming time.

Species List for Eastern Long Island

Arethusa bulbosa   **dragon's-mouth**
Calopogon tuberosus   **grass-pink**
Corallorhiza maculata var. *maculata*   **spotted coralroot**
Cypripedium acaule   **pink lady's-slipper, or moccasin flower**
Epipactis helleborine   **broad-leaved helleborine***
Goodyera pubescens   **downy rattlesnake orchis**
Goodyera tesselata   **checkered rattlesnake orchis**
Isotria verticillata   **large whorled pogonia**
Liparis loeselii   **Loesel's twayblade, or fen orchis**

Listera australis   **southern twayblade**
Listera cordata   **heart-leaved twayblade**
Malaxis bayardii   **Bayard's adder's-mouth**
Malaxis unifolia   **green adder's-mouth**
Platanthera blephariglottis var. *conspicua*   **southern white fringed orchis**
Platanthera ciliaris   **orange (yellow) fringed orchis**
Platanthera clavellata var. *clavellata*   **little club-spur orchis**
Platanthera cristata   **orange (yellow) crested orchis**
Platanthera flava var. *herbiola*   **northern tubercled orchis**
Platanthera lacera   **green fringed orchis, or ragged orchis**
Platanthera pallida   **pale fringed orchis**
Platanthera psycodes   **small purple fringed orchis**
Pogonia ophioglossoides   **rose pogonia**
Spiranthes cernua   **nodding ladies'-tresses**
Spiranthes lacera var. *lacera*   **northern slender ladies'-tresses**
Spiranthes lacera var. *gracilis*   **southern slender ladies'-tresses**
Spiranthes ochroleuca   **yellow ladies'-tresses**
Spiranthes praecox   **giant ladies'-tresses**
Spiranthes tuberosa   **little ladies'-tresses**
Spiranthes vernalis   **grass-leaved ladies'-tresses**
Tipularia discolor   **crane-fly orchis**

* = introduced species

A key is a means for identifying an unknown specimen. The principles used in keying are very simple. The key consists of a series of couplets. Each couplet offers two descriptions of some plant character. For example, you may be asked to choose whether leaves are present or absent at flowering time; or whether the leaves are basal or cauline. If you choose correctly (be sure to read both halves of the couplet before making your choice!) and proceed through the key as directed, the key will lead you to the correct name of the plant you are examining. Illustrations are located throughout the keys to help you in making your determinations.

Choose the specimen you wish to identify carefully. Look for a typical plant—neither the largest nor the smallest. This key is designed so that you can use it without picking any flowers, although detailed examinations will be necessary to distinguish a few similar species. Measurements have been kept to a minimum, as has the use of color to characterize flowers. Be aware that many of the species have white-flowered forms. These usually occur with the typical color form.

The key will help you identify the genus of your unknown orchid. Genera with multiple species have their own keys at the beginning of the genus description.

Before you use the key you should always note the following:

1. Placement and quantity of leaves: basal vs. cauline; opposite vs. alternate; one, two, or more
2. Placement and quantity of flowers: terminal vs. axillary; single vs. multiple
3. Geographic location and habitat

If you have never used a key before, the following exercise may be helpful. Imagine you are trying to identify a **pink lady's-slipper**, *Cypripedium acaule*. Start with couplet 1 of the key to the genera:

1a. Leaves present at flowering time . . . 2
1b. Leaves absent at flowering time . . . 24
which takes you to couplet 2

2a. Leaves basal (or apparently so) . . . 3
2b. Leaves cauline . . . 12
which takes you to couplet 3

3a. Single leaf . . . 4
3b. Two or more leaves . . . 8
which takes you to couplet 8

8a. Leaves two, opposite . . . 9
8b. Leaves more than two, basal rosette . . . 11
which takes you to couplet 9

9a. Leaves ascending . . . **Liparis**
9b. Leaves lying flat, or nearly so, on the ground . . . 10
which takes you to couplet 10

10a. Leaves smooth . . . **Platanthera**
10b. Leaves hairy . . . **Cypripedium**
*which takes you to the identity of the genus: **Cypripedium***

To determine which species of **Cypripedium** you have, turn to the species key for **Cypripedium** and follow the same procedure. Keys are not difficult to use if you take your time, learn the vocabulary, and hone your observational skills. And, as with any endeavor, the more you key out species the easier it becomes.

Key to the Genera

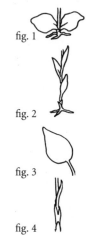

1a. Leaves present at flowering time . . . 2
1b. Leaves absent at flowering time . . . 24

2a. Leaves basal (or apparently so) (fig. 1) . . . 3
2b. Leaves cauline (fig. 2) . . . 12

3a. Single leaf . . . 4
3b. Two or more leaves . . . 8

4a. Single flower . . . 5
4b. Multiple flowers . . . 6

5a. Leaf oval with distinct petiole (fig. 3) . . . **Calypso**, p. 42
5b. Leaf linear, appressed to stem (fig. 4) . . . **Arethusa**, p. 38

fig. 1

fig. 2

fig. 3

fig. 4

6a. Leaf smooth . . . 7
6b. Leaf wrinkled . . . **Aplectrum**, p. 36

7a. Leaf broadly ovate (fig. 5), flowers white to pink . . . **Amerorchis**, p. 34
7b. Leaf narrowly ovate (fig. 6), flowers greenish . . . **Platanthera**, p. 130

fig. 5

fig. 6

8a. Leaves two, opposite . . . 9
8b. Leaves more than two, basal rosette . . . 11

9a. Leaves ascending . . . **Liparis**, p. 105
9b. Leaves lying flat, or nearly so, on the ground . . . 10

10a. Leaves smooth . . . **Platanthera**, p. 130
10b. Leaves hairy . . . **Cypripedium**, p. 61

11a. Leaves entirely green, oblong to broadly ovate . . . **Spiranthes**, p. 175
11b. Leaves pale to dark green with white marbling, elliptic . . . **Goodyera**, p. 85

12a. Single leaf . . . 13
12b. Multiple leaves . . . 15

13a. Single flower . . . 14
13b. Multiple flowers . . . **Malaxis**, p. 123

fig. 7

14a. Leaf linear (fig. 7) . . . **Arethusa**, p. 38
14b. Leaf ovate (fig. 8) . . . **Pogonia**, p. 172

15a. Leaves opposite . . . 16
15b. Leaves alternate . . . 17

fig. 8

16a. Leaves two . . . **Listera**, p. 111
16b. Leaves more than two, whorled . . . **Isotria**, p. 99

17a. Lip uppermost (fig. 9) . . . **Calopogon**, p. 40
17b. Lip lowermost . . . 18

fig. 9

18a. Lip in the form of a pouch (fig. 10) . . . **Cypripedium**, p. 61
18b. Lip otherwise . . . 19

fig. 10

19a. Leaves rounded, one to one and a half times longer than wide . . . 20
19b. Leaves oblong to linear, three or more times longer than wide . . . 21

20a. Leaves small and scalelike (fig. 11) . . . **Triphora**, p. 200
20b. Leaves otherwise . . . **Galearis**, p. 82

fig. 11

21a. Leaves grasslike (fig. 12) . . . **Spiranthes**, p. 175
21b. Leaves otherwise . . . 22

22a. Lip oval, strongly saccate (fig. 13) . . . **Epipactis**, p. 77
22b. Lip otherwise . . . 23

23a. Lip with a square notch (fig. 14) . . . **Coeloglossum**, p. 44
23b. Lip otherwise . . . 24

fig. 12

24a. Lip three parted; dense bright purple flowers (historical
introduction) . . . **Gymnadenia**, p. 96
24b. Lip otherwise . . . **Platanthera**, p. 130

fig. 13

25a. Flowers with a spur (fig. 15) . . . **Tipularia**, p. 198
25b. Flowers without a spur . . . 26

fig. 14

26a. Single flower . . . **Arethusa**, p. 38
26b. Multiple flowers . . . 27

fig. 15

27a. Stems green (chlorophyll present) . . . **Spiranthes**, p. 175
27b. Stems not green (chlorophyll lacking) . . . **Corallorhiza**,
p. 47

The orchid species of Maine, New Hampshire, Vermont, Massachusetts, Rhode Island, Connecticut, New York, and adjacent Pennsylvania and New Jersey are presented in alphabetical order by scientific name. The nomenclature is based on my *Checklist of the Orchids of North America North of Mexico* (1995). The blooming dates and measurements given for each species are not precise, but they are accurate enough to help you determine the species. Range information is given first for the northeastern states. The references to Pennsylvania and New Jersey relate only to the northern tier of counties and not to the presence, or absence, of a species in other parts of those states. Parentheses around a state name indicate historical presence only, as does "h" next to an area on the distribution map. The range in North America is given below the regional range. An asterisk following the common name indicates an introduced species.

The designation "regionally significant species" indicates a species that is listed, by state Natural Heritage Programs, as Threatened or Endangered within the Northeast. A "nationally significant species" is one listed as Threatened or Endangered throughout its U.S. range. The designation "Threatened" refers to a species listed as such by the U.S. Fish and Wildlife Service under the terms of the Endangered Species Act. Terms describing abundance are defined as follows:

rare	usually fewer than five known sites in the state, only a few individuals are present
local	few known sites, but these often have substantial populations
occasional	scattered throughout the region with populations of varying size
frequent	found, in suitable habitat, most of the time and in good numbers

Amerorchis rotundifolia (Banks ex Pursh) Hultén

Small Round-leaved Orchis

Maine, (Vermont, New York)
Alaska to Newfoundland, south to Minnesota and Maine

northern cedar swamps and woodlands
June 14–July 8

height: 9–25 cm   flowers: 3–10, 1.5–2 cm
white to pale pink with purple spotting

rare to local in northern Maine; historical in Vermont and New York

color photos 1–3

One of the rarest orchids in the region, this species is at the southern limit of its range. It is currently known from only a few sites in northern Maine, several of which are now under protected ownership through the Nature Conservancy. The species inhabits old, mossy cedar glades in undisturbed areas. It is not tolerant of logging operations or other major alterations to its home. **Eastern fairy-slipper**, *Calypso bulbosa* var. *americana*, is often found growing nearby. The white-flowered form, forma *beckettiae* (Boivin) Hultén, has not been found within our area.

nationally significant species

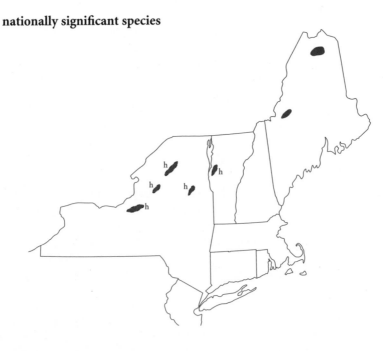

small round-leaved orchis

Aplectrum hyemale (Muhlenberg ex Willdenow) Torrey

Putty-root, or Adam and Eve

Vermont, Massachusetts, (Connecticut), New York, New Jersey
Minnesota to Massachusetts, south to Arkansas and Georgia

forma *pallidum* House: yellow-flowered form

rich mesic forests
May 20–June 10

height: 23–52 cm   flowers: 5–20, 0.75–2 cm
greenish yellow with madder-purple markings

rare in western Vermont and central Massachusetts, New York, and New
Jersey; historical in Connecticut

color photos 4–7

Formerly more abundant in the Northeast, this species is at the northern limit
of its range. It is presently known from only a very few sites in western New
England and in western and central New York and adjacent New Jersey.
Aplectrum is a frequently encountered orchid in the southeastern United
States, but it has always been less common in the Northeast. Nearly 90% of the
vouchered stations in our region have been extirpated.

regionally significant species

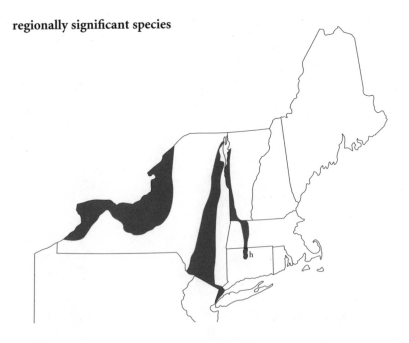

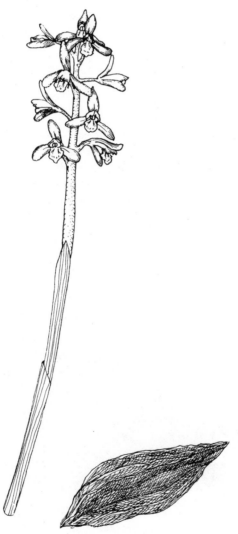

putty-root, or Adam and Eve

Arethusa bulbosa Linnaeus

Dragon's-mouth

New England, New York, Pennsylvania, New Jersey
Minnesota to Newfoundland, south to North Carolina

> forma *albiflora* Rand & Redfield: white-flowered form
> forma *subcaerulea* Rand & Redfield: lilac blue–flowered form

sphagnum bogs and wet meadows
May 20–July 15

height: 4–15 (extreme: 20) cm   flowers: 1 (rarely 2 or 3), 2.5–4 cm
rose-purple to brilliant pink

occasional in northern New England; local to rare in southern New England,
    New York, Pennsylvania, and New Jersey

color photos 8–10

One of the most beautiful of the bog orchids in North America, this species is
still present in large numbers in northern New England and in scattered local
colonies in southeastern New England and New York. Much of its former
habitat in southern New England has been destroyed in recent years, although
small, persistent stands can still be found near Boston and other major urban
areas.

regionally significant species

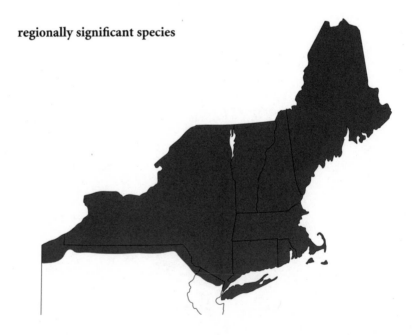

dragon's-mouth

Calopogon tuberosus (Linnaeus) Britton, Sterns & Poggenberg var. *tuberosus*

Grass-pink

New England, New York, Pennsylvania, New Jersey
Minnesota to Newfoundland, south to Texas and Florida

forma *albiflorus* Britton: white-flowered form

bogs, damp meadows
June 20–August 5

height: 10–52 cm   flowers: 3–10, 2.5–5 cm
pale lavender to brilliant pink

occasional throughout the region; locally abundant

color photos 11–14

Grass-pink, **dragon's-mouth**, *Arethusa bulbosa*, and **rose pogonia**, *Pogonia ophioglossoides*, are the three jewels of the open bog. Often growing in the same areas, they provide several weeks of late spring and early summer color. Of the three, *Calopogon* is the largest and showiest. It also grows in a wider variety of habitats. Several areas of wet roadside ditches in southern Maine are painted brilliant pink each July with thousands of stems of **grass-pink**. The dwarf plants with wider leaves that had been segregated as var. *latifolius* (St. John) Boivin have proven to be an ecological rather than a genetic variation. One other variety, var. *simpsonii* (Chapman) Magrath, occurs in southern Florida.

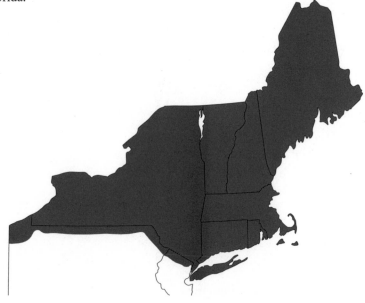

grass-pink

Calypso bulbosa (Linnaeus) Oakes var. *americana* (R. Brown) Luer

Eastern Fairy-slipper

Maine, (New Hampshire), Vermont, (New York)
Alaska to Newfoundland, south to the upper Great Lakes and northern New England; south in the Rocky Mountains

forma *albiflora* P.M. Brown: white-flowered form

northern cedar woods
May 20–June 14

height: 5–10 cm   flowers: 1, 2–3 cm
pale lavender-pink to deep pink with a yellow beard and darker markings on the lip

rare to local in Vermont and Maine; historical in New Hampshire and New York

color photos 15–18

This is one of the most sought after orchids in eastern North America. It prefers mature northern white cedar swamps and has declined in numbers as these areas have been cut for timber. It still can be found in scattered colonies in northern Vermont and northern Maine. A single record exists for New Hampshire. One of the last sightings in New York was on Valcour Island in Lake Champlain in 1949. The variety *bulbosa* is Eurasian; two additional varieties are in Japan and the Pacific Northwest.

regionally significant species

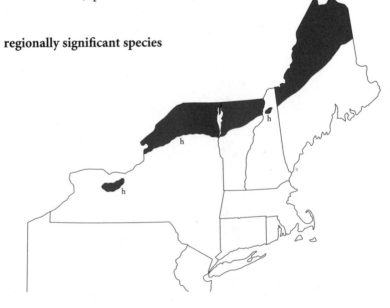

eastern fairy-slipper

Coeloglossum viride (Linnaeus) Hartman var. *virescens* (Muhlenberg) Luer

Long Bracted Green Orchis

New England, New York, Pennsylvania, New Jersey
Alaska to Newfoundland, south to Washington, New Mexico, Iowa, and North
  Carolina

rich mesic woodlands
May 15–August 18

height: 25–50 cm   flowers: 5–30, 0.5–1.25 cm
green with rosy purple overtones

occasional and scattered throughout the region

color photos 19, 20

Occasional and scattered in rich mesic woodlands, this green orchis is easily overlooked. It is somewhat capricious and not always reliable in the same spot each year. The rectangular, notched lip is distinctive and immediately separates this species from similar species of *Platanthera*. The variety *viride* is circumboreal.

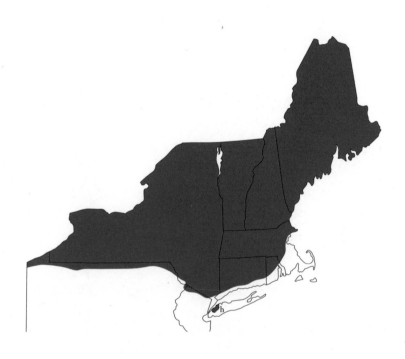

long bracted green orchis

Key to *Corallorhiza* (Coralroots)

Note: Unmarked lipped forms occur in all species.

1a. Lip striped . . . **striped coralroot**, *C. striata*
1b. Lip otherwise . . . 2

2a. Lip usually unspotted, spring flowering . . . **early coralroot**, *C. trifida*
2b. Lip spotted, summer and autumn flowering . . . 3

3a. Petals and sepals distinct, late spring to summer flowering . . . 4
3b. Petals and sepals indistinct, autumn flowering . . . 5

4a. Lip with parallel sides, mid to late summer flowering . . . **spotted coralroot**,
    C. maculata var. *maculata*
4b. Lip broadened toward apex, late spring to early summer
    flowering . . . **western spotted coralroot**, *C. maculata* var. *occidentalis*

5a. Lip prominent, flowers chasmogamous . . . **Pringle's autumn coralroot**,
    C. odontorhiza var. *pringlei*
5b. Lip not prominent, often undeveloped . . . **autumn coralroot**, *C. odontorhiza*
    var. *odontorhiza*

Corallorhiza maculata (Rafinesque) Rafinesque var. *maculata*

Spotted Coralroot

New England, New York, Pennsylvania, New Jersey
British Columbia to Newfoundland, south to California, Arizona, and New Mexico;
  south in the Appalachian Mountains and northern Georgia in the East

  forma *flavida* (C.H. Peck) Farwell: yellow-stemmed form
  forma *rubra* P.M. Brown: red-stemmed form

rich mesic and mixed forests
July 15–August 30

height: 20–50 cm   flowers: 5–20, 0.75–1 cm
tepals flesh-colored to red or yellow; lip white, spotted with madder-purple

local to occasional throughout the region

color photos 21–24

The eastern deciduous woodlands of midsummer to early autumn are scattered with **spotted coralroot**, our most frequently encountered coralroot. The variation in the stem color is similar to that seen in **western spotted coralroot**, but var. *maculata* plants are not as robust and tend not to grow in clumps.

spotted coralroot

Corallorhiza maculata (Rafinesque) Rafinesque
  var. *occidentalis* (Lindley) Ames

Western Spotted Coralroot

Maine, New Hampshire, Vermont, Massachusetts, New York
British Columbia to Newfoundland, south to California, Arizona, New Mexico,
  Minnesota, New England, and Virginia

forma *immaculata* (Peck) Howell: yellow spotless form
forma *intermedia* Farwell: brown-stemmed form
forma *punicea* (Bartlett) Weatherby & Adams: red-stemmed form

northern hardwoods and conifers
June 10–July 20

height: 20–50 cm   flowers: 10–70, 0.75–1.25 cm

tepals variously colored red to brown to yellow; lip white with reddish purple
  spots, or pure white in the forma *immaculata*

rare to local in northern counties; disjunct southward

color photos 25–28

Recently restored to its rightful status, but much rarer than the typical variety,
var. *occidentalis* occurs locally in northern New Hampshire and in scattered
colonies elsewhere in northern New England and New York. Disjunct stations
occur as far south as Virginia. The different color forms offer the orchid
enthusiast the challenge of finding a complete set. In June 1993 more than 300
stems were observed of forma *immaculata* near Mount Washington in northern New Hampshire.

western spotted coralroot

Corallorhiza odontorhiza (Willdenow) Nuttall var. *odontorhiza*

Autumn Coralroot

New England, New York, Pennsylvania, New Jersey
Minnesota to Maine, south to Oklahoma and Georgia

   forma *flavida* Wherry: yellow-stemmed form

rich mesic forests
August 28–September 30

height: 5–10 cm   flowers: 5–18, lip: 3–5 mm
lip white with purple spotting

rare to local throughout the region

color photos 29, 30

Uncommon but widespread throughout most of central and western New England, New York, and adjacent Pennsylvania and New Jersey in rich mesic forests, this species is easily overlooked because of its late blooming time and tiny, cleistogamous flowers.

autumn coralroot

Corallorhiza odontorhiza (Willdenow) Nuttall
  var. *pringlei* (Greenman) Freudenstein, ined.

Pringle's Autumn Coralroot

Connecticut, Massachusetts, Maine, Vermont
Iowa to Maine, south to Tennessee and North Carolina; Mexico

rich mesic forests
August 15–September 30

height: 5–15 cm   flowers: 3–12, lip: 4.5–10 mm
expanded white lip with purple markings

rare; occurs at the northern limits of var. *odontorhiza*

color photo 31

An extremely rare variety in the Northeast; the center of distribution is the lower Great Lakes. This variety was only recently described, although plants with showy, chasmogamous flowers have been known for some time.

Pringle's autumn coralroot

Corallorhiza striata Lindley var. *striata*

Striped Coralroot

New York
British Columbia to Quebec, south to California and New York

moist hardwoods and mixed forests
June 10–July 5

height: 15–45 cm   flowers: 5–20, 1–2 cm
pale coral stems; lip striped with cinnabar-red

rare

color photos 32, 33

This, the largest and showiest of the coralroots, is known in the Northeast only from central New York State. The species is more abundant to the west around the Great Lakes. Reported for Vermont but never vouchered. The only other variety, *vreelandii*, is found primarily in the western United States.

regionally significant species

striped coralroot

Corallorhiza trifida Chatelain

Early Coralroot

New England, New York, Pennsylvania, New Jersey
Alaska through Newfoundland, south to Oregon, the southern Rocky Mountains,
    eastern West Virginia, and New Jersey

swamps, bogs, rich woods
May 18–July 14

height: 7.5–15 cm   flowers: 0.6–1.25 cm
bright yellow stems; lip white

occasional in northern New England and New York; rare to local in southern
    areas

color photos 34, 35

Widespread throughout the northern and western areas in cool forests in all
but Rhode Island, this charming species is often the first orchid to bloom in
the spring. Its bright yellow stems are always a delight. Includes the variety
verna, which has proven to be variable over its range.

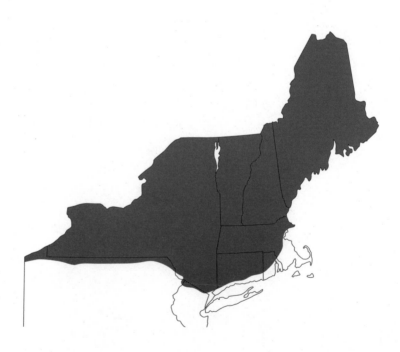

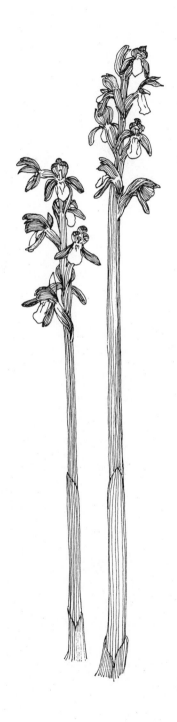

early coralroot

Key to *Cypripedium* (Lady's-slippers)

1a. Leaves basal . . . **pink lady's-slipper**, *C. acaule*
1b. Leaves cauline . . . 2

2a. Sepals and petals white, lip shades of pink . . . **showy lady's-slipper**, *C. reginae*
2b. Sepals and petals otherwise . . . 3

3a. Lip white . . . 4
3b. Lip yellow . . . 5

4a. Lip white, streaked with lavender; sepals 2 . . . **small white lady's-slipper**, *C. candidum*
4b. Lip veined and spotted with purple; sepals 3 . . . **ram's-head lady's-slipper**, *C. arietinum*

5a. Outer surface of uppermost sheathing bract (below the leaves) densely and conspicuously silvery pubescent when young (later sometimes glabrescent); flowers large to small, lip 20–54 mm long; sepals and petals variously marked with reddish brown or madder (dark purplish brown; rarely unmarked); scent moderate to faint, roselike or pungent musty . . . 6
5b. Outer surface of uppermost sheathing bract (below the leaves) sparsely and inconspicuously pubescent to glabrous when young; flowers small, lip 15–29 mm long; sepals and petals usually suffused with dark reddish brown or madder; scent intensely sweet; plants of calcareous fens and other mesic to limy wetlands; western and northern New England to the Great Lakes northward . . . **northern small yellow lady's-slipper**, *C. parviflorum* var. *makasin*

6a. Flowers commonly large, lip to 54 mm long, but very small in some northern plants; sepals and petals unmarked to spotted, striped, or reticulately marked with reddish brown or madder, rarely extensively blotched; plants of a variety of habitats, usually mesic to calcareous woodlands or open sites in limestone or gypsum; through the range of the species . . . **large yellow lady's-slipper**, *C. parviflorum* var. *pubescens*
6b. Flowers small, lip 22–34 mm long; sepals and petals usually densely and minutely spotted with dark reddish brown or madder appearing uniformly dark (rarely coarsely spotted and blotched); plants of dry, deciduous, more acidic sites than var. *pubescens*; southern New England to Kansas southward . . . **southern small yellow lady's-slipper**, *Cypripedium parviflorum* var. *parviflorum*

Couplets for *Cypripedium parviflorum* and its varieties adapted from those written by Charles J. Sheviak, Ph.D. Used by permission.

Cypripedium acaule Aiton

Pink Lady's-slipper, or Moccasin Flower

New England, New York, Pennsylvania, New Jersey
Northwest Territories to Newfoundland, south to Minnesota and Georgia

> forma *albiflorum* Rand & Redfield: white-flowered form
> forma *biflorum* P.M. Brown: two-flowered form

mixed and coniferous forests
May 15–July 25

height: 10–30 cm   flowers: 1 (rarely 2), 6–9 cm
pale rosy pink to deep raspberry

occasional to frequent in acid-soil areas throughout the region; rare to local in
 alkaline-soil areas

color photos 36–40

Perhaps the most familiar wild orchid in the Northeast. Large stands ranging
in size from several hundred to several thousand plants can be found. The
species occurs throughout all but the most alkaline areas. The forma *albiflorum* is more frequent northward.

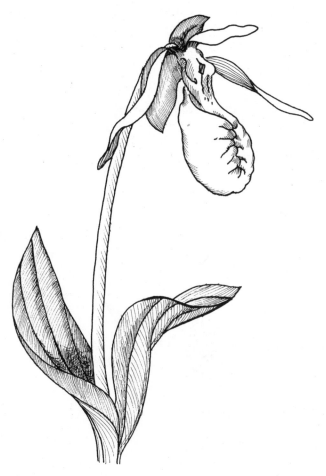

pink lady's-slipper, or moccasin flower

Cypripedium arietinum R. Brown

Ram's-head Lady's-slipper

Maine, New Hampshire, Vermont, Massachusetts, (Connecticut), New York
Manitoba to Nova Scotia, south to Minnesota and Massachusetts

forma *albiflorum* House: white-flowered form
forma *biflorum* P.M. Brown: two-flowered form

rich mesic forests; rare in alkaline bogs
May 10–June 18

height: 12–21 cm   flowers: 1 (rarely 2), 1–2 cm
white marked and veined with purple

rare to local throughout northern and central Maine, New Hampshire, Vermont, Massachusetts, and New York; historical in Connecticut; absent from Rhode Island

color photos 41–44

This, the smallest of our lady's-slippers, is becoming increasingly difficult to find in the Northeast. Alteration of habitat and vandalism have contributed to the decline. Vermont has several populations, but most of the other states have only one or two extant sites. This species is more abundant in the northern Great Lakes area.

nationally significant species

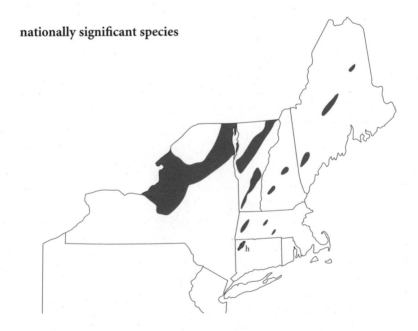

ram's-head lady's-slipper

Cypripedium candidum Muhlenberg ex Willdenow

Small White Lady's-slipper

New York, New Jersey
Saskatchewan to Minnesota and western New York, south to Missouri, Kentucky,
   and New Jersey

calcareous fens
May 12–June 8

height: 10–25 cm   flowers: 1–3, 2–4 cm
lip white with lavender inside; sepals purple

rare and local in west-central New York and northern New Jersey; extirpated
   in several historical sites

color photo 45

Known in the Northeast only from a few remnant populations in western New
York and northern New Jersey. Nearly all the sites where this charming little
lady's-slipper grows are under protection. The most notable site in New York
is owned by the Bergen Swamp Preservation Society, headquartered in
Rochester.

nationally significant species

small white lady's-slipper

Cypripedium parviflorum Salisbury var. *parviflorum*

Southern Small Yellow Lady's-slipper

Massachusetts, Connecticut, Rhode Island, New York, Pennsylvania, New Jersey
Kansas to Massachusetts, south to Louisiana and Georgia

neutral to acidic deciduous woodlands
May 15–June 10

height: 10–60 cm   flowers: 1–3, 2–4 cm
lip deep yellow with scarlet markings inside, often visible from the exterior;
petals and sepals suffused with dark chestnut–purple to brown

rare in southern New England, New York, and adjacent Pennsylvania and
New Jersey

color photos 46, 51

The recent taxonomic separation of the two **small yellow lady's-slippers** into
northern and southern varieties has solved an often confusing question. How
can the small-flowered, dark-petaled yellow lady's-slippers that occur in dry,
acid woods be the same as the similar plants in the typical calcareous wetlands? The answer is that they are not the same; nor are they gradations of the
large yellow, var. *pubescens*. Habitat, range, and the delicate roselike fragrance should be more than sufficient to identify this rare variety in southern
New England, the southern counties of New York, and adjacent Pennsylvania
and New Jersey.

regionally significant variety

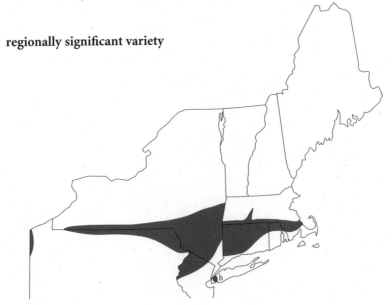

southern small yellow lady's-slipper

Cypripedium parviflorum Salisbury var. *makasin* (Farwell) Sheviak

Northern Small Yellow Lady's-slipper

Maine, New Hampshire, Vermont, Massachusetts, Connecticut, New York, Pennsylvania

British Columbia to northern California, east to Newfoundland, south to Pennsylvania; south in the Rocky Mountains

northern white cedar bogs and fens
May 24–July 18

height: 10–60 cm   flowers: 1–3, 3–5 cm
lip deep yellow with scarlet markings inside, often visible from the exterior; petals and sepals suffused with dark chestnut–purple to pale brown

local to occasional in northern New England, New York, and northwestern Pennsylvania

color photo 47

Although this variety superficially resembles var. *parviflorum*, its preferred habitats—cold, northern cedar bogs and swamps, and, farther west, the northern prairies—are as different as can be imagined. Its intense, sweet fragrance is also a good field key. The two varieties of **small yellow lady's-slippers** barely overlap in range, and never in habitat.

northern small yellow lady's-slipper

Cypripedium parviflorum Salisbury var. *pubescens* (Willdenow) Knight

Large Yellow Lady's-slipper

New England, New York, Pennsylvania, New Jersey
Alaska to Newfoundland, south to Louisiana and Georgia

rich mesic forest, edges of bogs and fens
May 10–July 1

height: 15–60 cm   flowers: 1–3 (rarely 4), 5–8 cm
lip pale to bright yellow with few scarlet markings inside; petals and sepals
   with a series of disconnected markings and with overall coloring from dark
   to light

local to occasional throughout the region

color photos 48–51

This is the classic yellow lady's-slipper so familiar to many wildflower lovers
and gardeners. Although it has declined dramatically in some areas in the past
25 years, it still can be found in rich mesic forests and swamps throughout the
Northeast. The fact that this is one of the few native orchids that can be
cultivated in the garden has led to its decline in the wild. All too often I visit
sites where once there were many plants and find only empty holes. Because
the plants do grow well under cultivation they can be purchased as propagated
plants; there is no need to rape the woodlands to get them.

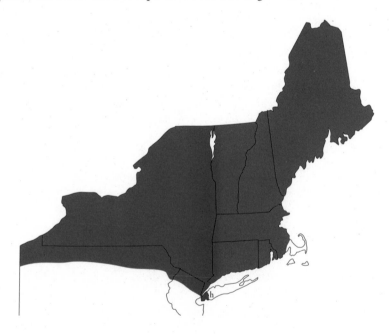

large yellow lady's-slipper

Cypripedium reginae Walter

Showy Lady's-slipper

Maine, New Hampshire, Vermont, Massachusetts, Connecticut, New York, Pennsylvania, New Jersey
Saskatchewan to Newfoundland, south to Iowa and northern Alabama

forma *albolabium* Fernald & Schubert: white-flowered form

calcareous wetlands
June 10–July 25

height: 30–80 cm   flowers: 1–3 (rarely 4), 5–12.5 cm
lip pink to rosy red; petals and sepals white

occasional in Vermont and upstate New York; local in Maine and Pennsylvania; rare to local in western New Hampshire, Massachusetts, northwestern Connecticut, northern New Jersey, and northwestern Pennsylvania

color photos 52–55

This is the largest and most impressive of our lady's-slippers, and perhaps of all the orchids in the Northeast. The spectacular white and pink flowers often grow to a height of 80 cm, and the flowers are frequently to 12.5 cm across. The plants favor open to lightly wooded calcareous swamps, often in the company of tamarack and black spruce. Like the **large yellow lady's-slipper**, this species also falls victim to collectors.

showy lady's-slipper

Cypripedium Hybrids

Cypripedium ✕*andrewsii* Fuller nm. *andrewsii*
Andrews' Hybrid Lady's-slipper
(*C. candidum* ✕ *C. parviflorum* var. *makasin*)
color photo 56

Cypripedium ✕*andrewsii* Fuller nm. *favillianum* (Curtis) Boivin
Faville's Hybrid Lady's-slipper
(*C. candidum* ✕ *C. parviflorum* var. *pubescens*)
color photo 57

Both hybrids are found as rare individuals in the very few areas where the parent species overlap in west-central New York State.

Key to *Epipactis* (Helleborines)

Inflorescence and ovaries pubescent, flowers cranberry red; plants of dry, sunny serpentines (northern Vermont) . . . **red helleborine**, *E. atrorubens*

Inflorescence and ovaries glabrous, flowers greenish white to shades of greenish pink, plants of various habitats and widely distributed . . . **broad-leaved helleborine**, *E. helleborine*

Epipactis atrorubens (Berber) Besser

Red Helleborine*

Vermont

exposed serpentine formations
July 25–August 18

height: 18–30 cm   flowers: 5–20, 0.75–1.5 cm
cranberry red

color photo 58

One of two European *Epipactis* species found in the Northeast, *E. atrorubens* was discovered in an abandoned serpentine quarry in northern Vermont in 1990. It is less likely to spread than *E. helleborine*, as its habitat preference is quite specific.

red helleborine

Epipactis helleborine (Linnaeus) Cranz

Broad-leaved Helleborine*

New England, New York, Pennsylvania, New Jersey
Eastern United States, eastern Canada, and scattered in western North America

> forma *alba* (Webster) Boivin: white-flowered form
> forma *luteola* P.M. Brown: yellow-flowered form
> forma *monotropoides* (Mousley) Scoggin: albino form
> forma *variegata* (Webster) Boivin: variegated form
> forma *viridens* A. Gray: green-flowered form

found in a variety of habitats, from rich woodlands to cracks in sidewalks;
   typically a lime lover
June 28–October 10

height: 5–84 cm   flowers: 15–50, 1–3 cm
green-yellow often suffused with rosy pink

color photos 59–62

This common European species was first introduced to North America in 1888 near Rochester, New York. It has since spread throughout the Northeast and can now be found all the way eastward to downtown Boston and northward to Nova Scotia and Newfoundland. The forms other than forma *viridens* are exceedingly rare and are represented in very few collections.

broad-leaved helleborine

Galearis spectabilis (Linnaeus) Rafinesque

Showy Orchis

New England, New York, Pennsylvania, New Jersey
Minnesota to Maine, south to Arkansas and Georgia

> forma *gordinierii* (House) Whiting & Catling: white-flowered form
> forma *willeyi* (Seymour) P.M. Brown: pink-flowered form

rich mesic forests
May 10–June 25

height: 10–15 cm   flowers: 3–12, 1.5–2 cm
lip white; sepals and petals lavender purple

rare to local throughout the region

color photos 63–66

This an orchid is typical of the rich mesic forests of central and western New England and New York. It is occasional to frequent in Vermont, New York, Pennsylvania, and New Jersey; local in Massachusetts and Connecticut; and rare in New Hampshire, Maine, and Rhode Island.

showy orchis

1. Small round-leaved orchis
Amerorchis rotundifolia

2. Small round-leaved orchis
Amerorchis rotundifolia

3. Small round-leaved orchis
Amerorchis rotundifolia

4. Putty-root
Aplectrum hyemale

An asterisk (*) indicates that the species is introduced.

6. Putty-root, winter leaf
Aplectrum hyemale

5. Putty-root
Aplectrum hyemale

7. Putty-root, yellow-flowered form
Aplectrum hyemale forma *pallidum*

8. Dragon's-mouth
Arethusa bulbosa

9. Dragon's-mouth, white-flowered form
Arethusa bulbosa forma *albiflora*

10. Dragon's-mouth, lilac blue–flowered form
Arethusa bulbosa forma *subcaerulea*

11. Grass-pink
Calopogon tuberosus var. *tuberosus*

12. Grass-pink, white-flowered form
Calopogon tuberosus var. *tuberosus*
forma *albiflorus*

13. Grass-pink, bicolored variant
Calopogon tuberosus var. *tuberosus*

14. Grass-pink, dwarf variant
Calopogon tuberosus var. *tuberosus*
(formerly var. *latifolius*)

15. Eastern fairy-slipper
Calypso bulbosa var. *americana*

16. Eastern fairy-slipper
Calypso bulbosa var. *americana*

17. Eastern fairy-slipper
Calypso bulbosa var. *americana*

18. Eastern fairy-slipper, white-flowered form
Calypso bulbosa var. *americana* forma *albiflora*

19. Long bracted green orchis
Coeloglossum viride var. *virescens*

20. Long bracted green orchis.
Coeloglossum viride var. *virescens*

21. Spotted coralroot
Corallorhiza maculata var. *maculata*

22. Spotted coralroot
Corallorhiza maculata var. *maculata*

23. Spotted coralroot, yellow-stemmed form
Corallorhiza maculata var. *maculata*
forma *flavida*

24. Spotted coralroot, red-stemmed form
Corallorhiza maculata var. *maculata*
forma *rubra*

25. Western spotted coralroot
Corallorhiza maculata var. *occidentalis*

26. Western spotted coralroot
Corallorhiza maculata var. *occidentalis*

27. Western spotted coralroot, yellow spotless form
Corallorhiza maculata var. *occidentalis* forma *immaculata*

28. Western spotted coralroot, yellow spotless form
Corallorhiza maculata var. *occidentalis* forma *immaculata*

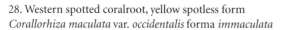

30. Autumn coralroot, yellow-stemmed form
Corallorhiza odontorhiza var. *odontorhiza*
forma *flavida*

29. Autumn coralroot
Corallorhiza odontorhiza var. *odontorhiza*

31. Pringle's autumn coralroot
Corallorhiza odontorhiza var. *pringlei*

32. Striped coralroot
Corallorhiza striata var. *striata*

33. Striped coralroot
Corallorhiza striata var. *striata*

34. Early coralroot
Corallorhiza trifida

36. Pink lady's-slipper
Cypripedium acaule

35. Early coralroot
Corallorhiza trifida

37. Pink lady's-slipper
Cypripedium acaule

38. Pink lady's-slipper, pale-flowered variant
Cypripedium acaule

39. Pink lady's-slipper, white-flowered form
(an unusual dwarf clump)
Cypripedium acaule forma *albiflorum*

40. Pink lady's-slipper, two-flowered form
Cypripedium acaule forma *biflorum*

41. Ram's-head lady's-slipper
Cypripedium arietinum

42. Ram's-head lady's-slipper
Cypripedium arietinum

43. Ram's-head lady's-slipper, typical (left)
and white-flowered form
Cypripedium arietinum and *C. arietinum*
forma *albiflorum*

44. Ram's-head lady's-slipper, two-flowered form
Cypripedium arietinum forma *biflorum*

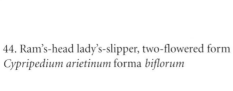

45. Small white lady's-slipper
Cypripedium candidum

46. Southern small yellow lady's-slipper
Cypripedium parviflorum var. *parviflorum*

48. Large yellow lady's-slipper
Cypripedium parviflorum var. *pubescens*

47. Northern small yellow lady's-slipper
Cypripedium parviflorum var. *makasin*

49. Large yellow lady's-slipper
Cypripedium parviflorum var. *pubescens*

50. Large yellow lady's-slipper,
horizontal petaled variant of northern fens
Cypripedium parviflorum var. *pubescens*

52. Showy lady's-slipper
Cypripedium reginae

51. Large yellow lady's-slipper (left)
and southern small yellow lady's-slipper
Cypripedium parviflorum var. *pubescens*
and *C. parviflorum* var. *parviflorum*

53. Showy lady's-slipper
Cypripedium reginae

54. Showy lady's-slipper
Cypripedium reginae

55. Showy lady's-slipper, white-flowered form
Cypripedium reginae forma *albolabium*

56. Andrews' hybrid lady's-slipper
Cypripedium ×*andrewsii* nm. *andrewsii*

57. Faville's hybrid lady's-slipper
Cypripedium ×andrewsii nm. *favillianum*

58. Red helleborine*
Epipactis atrorubens

59. Broad-leaved helleborine*
Epipactis helleborine

60. Broad-leaved helleborine,
yellow-flowered form*
Epipactis helleborine forma *luteola*

61. Broad-leaved helleborine, albino form*
Epipactis helleborine forma *monotropoides*

62. Broad-leaved helleborine,
green-flowered form*
Epipactis helleborine forma *viridens*

63. Showy orchis
Galearis spectabilis

64. Showy orchis
Galearis spectabilis

Key to *Goodyera* (Rattlesnake Orchises)

1a. Flowers in a dense spike . . . 2
1b. Flowers in a lax spike . . . 3

2a. Spike one sided . . . **giant rattlesnake orchis**, *G. oblongifolia*
2b. Spike otherwise . . . **downy rattlesnake orchis**, *G. pubescens*

3a. Spike one sided . . . **lesser rattlesnake orchis**, *G. repens*
3b. Spike spiraled . . . **checkered rattlesnake orchis**, *G. tesselata*

Goodyera oblongifolia Rafinesque

Giant Rattlesnake Orchis

Maine
Southern Alaska to Newfoundland, south to Minnesota, the upper Great Lakes, and
Maine; California and New Mexico; Mexico

forma *reticulata* (Boivin) P.M. Brown: reticulated-leaf form

second-growth mixed hardwoods
August 3–24

height: 22–35 cm   flowers: 12–30, 5 mm
tawny to white

rare in northern Aroostook County, Maine

color photos 67–70

Known only from Aroostook County in northernmost Maine, this disjunct
population is near the southeastern limit of the range for the species.

regionally significant species

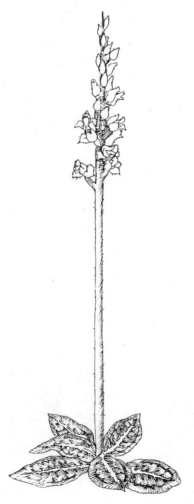

giant rattlesnake orchis

Goodyera pubescens (Willdenow) R. Brown

Downy Rattlesnake Orchis

New England, New York, Pennsylvania, New Jersey
Ontario to Nova Scotia, south to Arkansas and South Carolina

mixed forests, usually acidic soils
July 20–August 25

height: 16–25 cm   flowers: 2–70, 3–5 mm
white; covered with copious hairs

local in northern New England and New York; occasional to frequent in
southern regions

color photos 71–73

Known from all nine northeastern states, this is a distinctive species of the
southern and central oak-pine forests. It is locally abundant in southern New
England, New York, and adjacent Pennsylvania and New Jersey, but becomes
increasingly rare northward. Absent from the far northern counties.

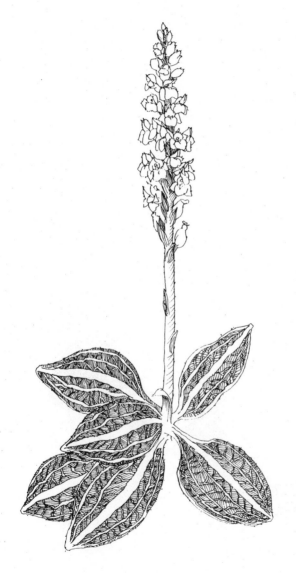

downy rattlesnake orchis

Goodyera repens (Linnaeus) R. Brown forma *ophioides* (Fernald) P.M. Brown

Lesser Rattlesnake Orchis

Maine, New Hampshire, Vermont, Massachusetts, (Connecticut), New York, Pennsylvania
Alaska to Newfoundland, south to Wyoming, the southern Rocky Mountains, and the southern Appalachian Mountains

cool coniferous forests
July 8–August 22

height: 6–12 cm   flowers: 8–15, 2–3 mm
milky white

occasional in northern New England and New York; absent from Rhode Island; historical in Connecticut; rare in southern areas

color photos 74, 75

This species, the smallest of the rattlesnake orchises, is occasional in northern New York and northern New England and increasingly rare southward. Only the forma *ophioides*, with its dark green and silver marbled leaves, grows in our region. The typical *G. repens*, with plain leaves, is a northern plant.

lesser rattlesnake orchis

Goodyera tesselata Loddiges

Checkered Rattlesnake Orchis

New England, New York, Pennsylvania, New Jersey
Ontario to Newfoundland, south to Minnesota and Maryland

mixed forests
July 15–September 25

height: 8–18 cm   flowers: 12–20, 3–4 mm
dusky white

occasional to frequent in northern areas; local in Massachusetts and Connecticut; rare southward

color photo 76

This rather unassuming wild orchid has neither the charm of *G. repens* nor the beauty of *G. pubescens*. It is rare and local (or absent) in the southern counties and becomes increasingly frequent to the north. It originated, historically, as a hybrid between *G. oblongifolia* and *G. repens*.

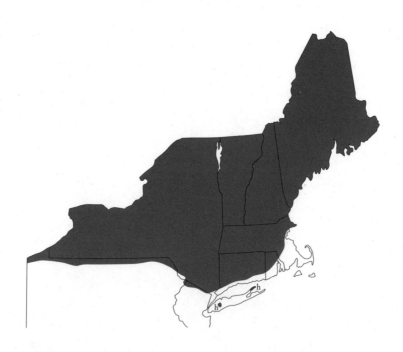

checkered rattlesnake orchis

Goodyera Hybrids

G. pubescens × *G. tesselata* (color photos 77, 78)
G. repens × *G. tesselata*
G. oblongifolia × *G. tesselata*
G. oblongifolia × *G. repens*

Goodyera hybrids are relatively rare, but look for them where two species occur together. Hybrids generally blend the qualities of their parents in a fairly obvious manner; for example, the leaves favoring one and the inflorescence the other. Hybrids of *G. pubescens* × *G. tesselata* occasionally have large, plain leaves and are mistaken for *G. oblongifolia.*

Gymnadenia conopsea (Linnaeus) R. Brown

Fragrant Orchis*

(Connecticut)

June

height: 25–50 cm   flowers: 18–45, 3–5 mm
brilliant purple

color photo 79

This European species was found once in Litchfield, Connecticut, but apparently did not persist. It is a common orchid of roadsides and meadows in many European countries.

fragrant orchis

Key to *Isotria* (Whorled Pogonias)

Sepals greenish yellow and one and a half times as long as the petals or shorter . . . **small whorled pogonia,** *I. medeoloides*

Sepals purple and two or more times as long as the petals . . . **large whorled pogonia,** *I. verticillata*

Isotria medeoloides (Pursh) Rafinesque

Small Whorled Pogonia

Maine, New Hampshire, (Vermont), Massachusetts, Connecticut, Rhode Island, (New York), New Jersey
Michigan to Maine, south to Missouri and Georgia

various wooded habitats, favoring beech and mixed conifers and hardwoods; often near seasonal runoff
May 25–July 6

height: 8–12 cm in bloom, 10–15 cm in fruit; flowers: 1–2, 1.5–2.5 cm greenish yellow petals and sepals; lip white

rare to local in the Northeast; concentrated in central and eastern New Hampshire and southwestern Maine; historical in Vermont and New York

color photos 80–82

This was one of the first orchids to be listed by the federal government under the Endangered Species Act. Although very rare, often known from a single station or even a single plant elsewhere in eastern North America, it can be locally abundant in New Hampshire and western Maine. Both states have sites with an excess of several thousand plants. The species occurred historically in New York and Vermont, and was once thought to be one of the rarest in North America, but ardent searching by both professionals and amateurs turned up many new sites.

Threatened

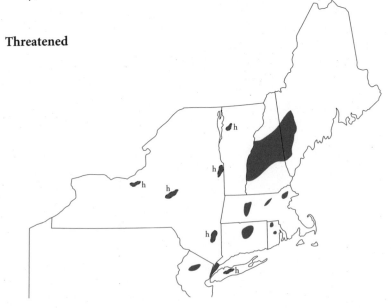

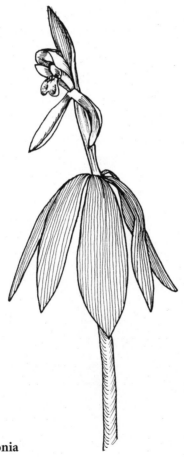

small whorled pogonia

Isotria verticillata (Willdenow) Rafinesque

Large Whorled Pogonia

New England, New York, Pennsylvania, New Jersey
Michigan to Maine, south to Texas and Florida

acidic and basic deciduous forests
May 15–June 18

height: 15–20 cm in bloom, 17–24 cm in fruit; flowers: 1–2, 4–7 cm
purplish green sepals and petals; lip white

rare in northern New England; occasional in southern New England, New
York, and adjacent Pennsylvania and New Jersey

color photos 83–86

This species has a very curious distribution in New England. Except for a
very large stand (several thousand plants) in northwestern Vermont near
Burlington, it is one of northern New England's rarest orchids. But the minute
you cross the state line into Massachusetts it becomes fairly frequent. In
southern New York State, Massachusetts, Rhode Island, and Connecticut it is
frequent to common in the predominant oak-pine woodlands.

large whorled pogonia

Key to *Liparis* (Twayblades)

Flowers chocolate-purple; plants of rich woodlands . . . **lily-leaved twayblade,**
  L. liliifolia

Flowers yellow-green; plants of moist areas . . . **Loesel's twayblade, or fen orchis,**
  L. loeselii

Liparis liliifolia (Linnaeus) Richard

Lily-leaved Twayblade

Vermont, Massachusetts, Connecticut, Rhode Island, New York, Pennsylvania, New Jersey
Minnesota to Vermont and Massachusetts, south to Arkansas and Georgia

forma *viridiflora* Wadmond: green-flowered form

rich mesic forests, often on calcareous soils
June 9–July 15

height: 9–17 cm   flowers: 12–78, 1–2 cm
lip chocolate-purple; petals and sepals green

local throughout southern areas; rare and scattered in Vermont and central New York

color photos 87–89

This large, handsome orchid of rich mesic forests and streamsides is one of the more elusive species in the Northeast. It has been vouchered and is extant in southern New England, Vermont (rare), New York, and adjacent Pennsylvania and New Jersey.

lily-leaved twayblade

Liparis loeselii (Linnaeus) Richard

Loesel's Twayblade, or Fen Orchis

New England, New York, Pennsylvania, New Jersey
Manitoba to Nova Scotia, south to Mississippi and the southern Appalachian
  Mountains; disjunct in Washington and Montana

damp gravels, bogs, ditches, and seepage areas
June 8–August 19

height: 3–15 cm   flowers: 3–15, 0.5–1 cm
yellow-green

occasional throughout the region

color photos 90, 91

The **fen orchis** is one of the few species shared by the northeastern United
States and northern Europe. Although rare in Europe, it is common in our
region, having been vouchered from every county in New England, most of
New York, and locally in adjacent Pennsylvania and New Jersey. In northern
New England plants can occur by the thousands in wet roadside ditches, damp
gravel pits, and, less frequently, bogs and swamps.

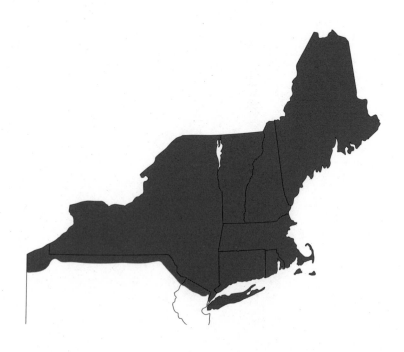

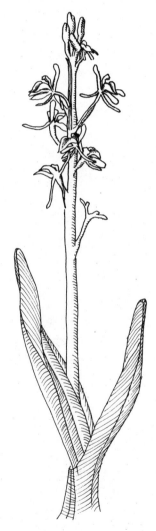

Loesel's twayblade, or fen orchis

Key to *Listera* (Twayblades)

1a. Lip deeply cleft, to more than half its length . . . 2
1b. Lip shallowly cleft, to less than half its length . . . 3

2a. Lip about twice as long as petals . . . **heart-leaved twayblade**, *L. cordata*
2b. Lip about four times as long as petals . . . **southern twayblade**, *L. australis*

3a. Lip with parallel sides, auricled at base . . . **auricled twayblade**, *L. auriculata*
3b. Lip tapered from summit to base, not auricled at base . . . 4

4a. Leaves rounded, usually longer than the peduncle of the raceme; plants of
   northern cool mossy woods and streamsides . . . **broad-lipped twayblade**,
   L. convallarioides
4b. Leaves kidney shaped, much shorter than the peduncle of the raceme; plants
   of northern New Jersey and Pennsylvania southward in wet woods and
   thickets . . . **Small's twayblade**, *L. smallii*

Listera auriculata Wiegand

Auricled Twayblade

Maine, New Hampshire, Vermont, New York
Ontario to Newfoundland, south to Michigan and Maine

  forma *trifolia* (Lepage) Lepage: three-leaved form

moist woods and alder thickets
June 25–August 5

height: 2–4.5 cm   flowers: 4–15, 0.5–7.5 mm
watery green

rare throughout the region

color photos 92, 93

The **auricled twayblade** superfically resembles the more frequently encountered **broad-lipped twayblade**, *L. convallarioides*, and the two species often occupy similar habitat. Careful examination of the lip should aid in identification. Although historical sites are scattered through most of northern Maine, only a few sites are extant. Northern New Hampshire, Vermont, and New York each have but one or two localities for this species.

nationally significant species

broad-lipped
twayblade

auricled twayblade

Listera australis Lindley

Southern Twayblade

Vermont, New York, Pennsylvania
Quebec to Nova Scotia, south to Arkansas and Florida

    forma *trifolia* P.M. Brown: three-leaved form

sphagnum bogs
May 25–July 10

height: 4–8 cm   flowers 8–20, 0.75–1.2 cm
lip rusty red with a green spot in the center

rare to local

color photos 94, 95

The **southern twayblade** is known in New England from two sites in northern Vermont, and in New York from several widely separated localities in the western and central parts of the state to eastern Long Island. It is rare in northern Pennsylvania. In color it resembles the reddish green sphagnum mosses in which it frequently grows, and it is easily overlooked.

nationally significant species

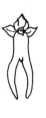

heart-leaved
twayblade

southern twayblade

Listera convallarioides (Swartz) Nuttall

Broad-lipped Twayblade

Maine, New Hampshire, Vermont, (New York)
British Columbia to Newfoundland, south to California, Wyoming, and northern
New England

forma *trifolia* P.M. Brown: three-leaved form

streamsides, swales, swampy woods
June 12–August 20

height: 4–15 cm   flowers: 5–15, 0.75–1.25 cm
watery green

local in central and northern Maine, New Hampshire, Vermont, and New
York

color photos 96–98

Locally abundant in northern New England (and formerly northeastern New
York), but absent from southern New England and the southern counties of
New York, it favors mossy rills and streamsides. It is not unusal to find large
colonies with several hundred plants packed in like a ground cover. Northern
Aroostook County, Maine, and northeastern Vermont are home to several
large stands.

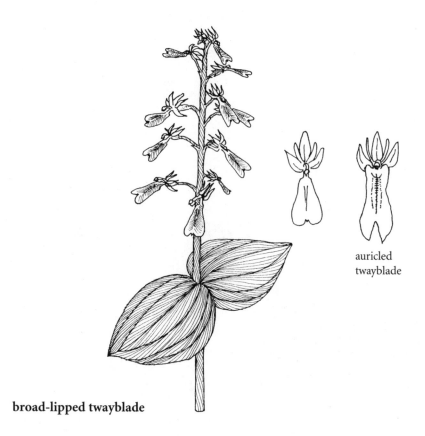

auricled
twayblade

broad-lipped twayblade

Listera cordata (Linnaeus) R. Brown var. *cordata*

Heart-leaved Twayblade

Maine, New Hampshire, Vermont, Massachusetts, (Connecticut, Rhode Island),
 New York, Pennsylvania, New Jersey
Alaska to Newfoundland, south to California, Rocky Mountain New Mexico, and
 Appalachian North Carolina

forma *disjuncta* Lepage: alternate-leaved form
forma *trifolia* P.M. Brown: three-leaved form
forma *variegata* P.M. Brown: variegated-leaf form
forma *viridens* P.M. Brown: green-flowered form

wet woods, often with northern white cedar
May 10–August 4

height: 4–8 cm   flowers: 8–17, 0.50–0.75 cm
copper-red

occasional in northern New England and New York; rare in southern New
 England and adjacent Pennsylvania and New Jersey

color photos 99–104

This little orchid is frequently encountered in the northern white cedar
swamps of northern New England and New York, and more rarely among the
Atlantic white cedar swamps of southeastern New England and Long Island.

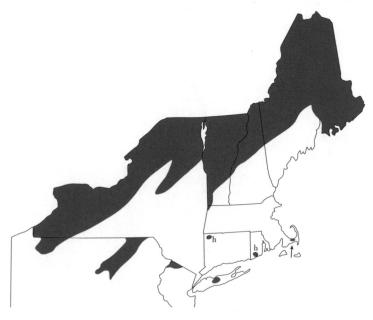

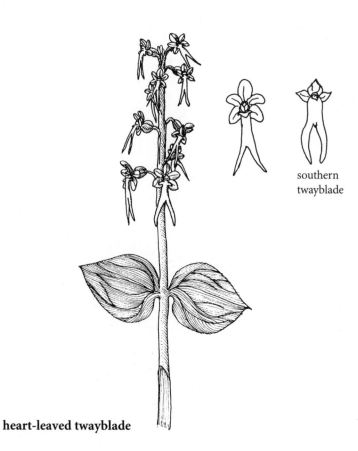

southern
twayblade

heart-leaved twayblade

Listera smallii Wiegand

Small's Twayblade

New Jersey
northern New Jersey, Pennsylvania to Georgia

wet woods
July 3–July 24

height: 10–30 cm   flowers: 4–12, 6–12 mm
yellow-beige to purple-brown

rare

color photo 105

This is the rarest twayblade in the Northeast, known only from Sussex County in northern New Jersey, not far from New York. The main body of distribution is from southwestern Pennsylvania south to Georgia. The New Jersey site is a good example of a disjunct population. Look for this species in similar habitat in adjacent Pennsylvania and New York.

regionally significant species

Small's twayblade

Listera Hybrid

Listera ×*veltmanii* Case

Veltman's Hybrid Twayblade

(*L. auriculata* × *L. convallarioides*)

color photo 106

The hybrid, first described from northern Michigan by Fred Case, has proven to occur wherever both parents grow together. It may resemble either parent with only minor variations.

Key to *Malaxis* (Adder's-mouths)

1a. Flowers on pedicles . . . 2
1b. Flowers sessile . . . **white adder's-mouth**, *M. brachypoda*

2a. Inflorescence elongate at maturity; lower flowers persistent when upper ones are prime; plants of drier habitats, often coastal sand plains or similar habitats . . . **Bayard's adder's-mouth**, *M. bayardii*
2b. Inflorescence broad at maturity; lower flowers withered when upper ones are prime; plants of moister habitats . . . **green adder's-mouth**, *M. unifolia*

Malaxis bayardii Fernald

Bayard's Adder's-mouth

Massachusetts, (Rhode Island, Connecticut), New York, Pennsylvania, (New Jersey)

Nova Scotia; Ohio to Massachusetts, south to North Carolina

dry pine plains, barrens, and coastal plain cemeteries
June 18–September 8

height: 4–18 cm   flowers: 35–150, 2–4 mm
chartreuse green

rare, but perhaps simply overlooked in its habitat; distribution not well known

color photos 107, 108

Recently revalidated as a species, this diminutive green orchid is currently known from only six sites, four of them in the Northeast. Historically the species was vouchered from North Carolina, Virginia, New Jersey, and extensively from Pennsylvania, as well as from New England and New York. The largest stand known, of about 400 individuals, is on an abandoned wood road and the adjacent fieldsides on Cape Cod. Its similarity to *M. unifolia* causes problems in identification, but Paul Catling's 1991 article in *Lindleyana* (6[1]: 3–23) goes into great detail and supports all identification criteria. Plants in dry habitat that appear to be *M. unifolia* should be carefully examined to determine whether they are *M. bayardii*. Unless more sites are found, this is an excellent candidate for federal listing as Threatened or Endangered.

nationally significant species

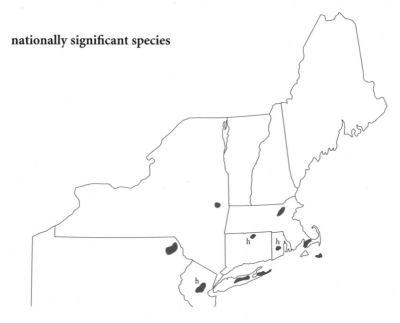

Bayard's adder's-mouth

Malaxis brachypoda (Gray) Fernald

White Adder's-mouth

Maine, New Hampshire, Vermont, Massachusetts, Connecticut, New York, New Jersey, Pennsylvania
Alaska to Newfoundland, south to California, Colorado, and Indiana to New Jersey

forma *bifolia* (Mousley) Fernald: two-leaved form

northern white cedar swamps and thickets, fens, calcareous ledges
June 5–August 20

height: 4–10 cm   flowers: 15–45, 2–3 mm
pale translucent green

rare to local in northern and western New England, New York, and adjacent Pennsylvania and New Jersey

color photos 109–111

Elusive and apparently declining, this slender, small orchid has a preference for cool mossy bogs, northern white cedar swamps, and calcareous seeps. It has even been found on wet shelves on marble outcrops. It is currently known from all the northeastern states but Rhode Island, where suitable habitat does not exist; it is more frequent, but by no means common, in the northern counties of New England.

regionally significant species

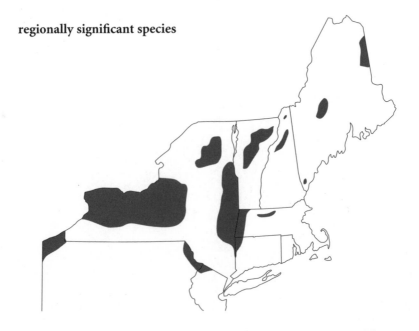

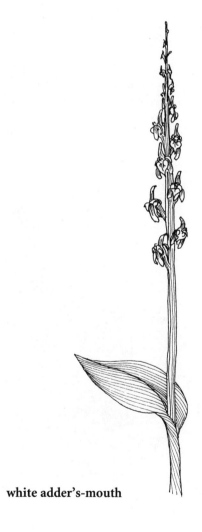

white adder's-mouth

Malaxis unifolia Michaux

Green Adder's-mouth

New England, New York, Pennsylvania, New Jersey
Manitoba to Newfoundland, south to Texas and Florida; Mexico

   forma *bifolia* (Mousley) Fernald: two-leaved form

damp meadows, bogs, open thickets
June 5–September 16

height: 2–10 cm   flowers: 15–70, 2–4 mm
lime green

formerly widespread throughout the Northeast; currently difficult to find,
   perhaps overlooked

color photos 112–114

This is one of the few species vouchered from every county in New England,
and nearly every county in New York and adjacent Pennsylvania and New
Jersey. Today it is hard to come by in some states and was only recently
rediscovered in Rhode Island. Succession and habitat destruction are the
primary reasons for its decline.

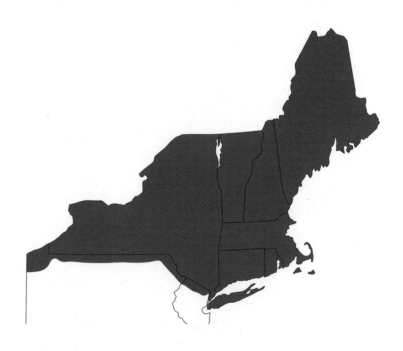

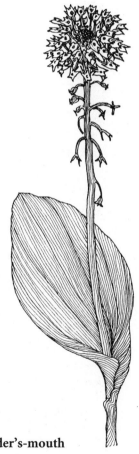

green adder's-mouth

Key to *Platanthera* (Fringed and Rein Orchises)

1a. Leaves basal . . . 2
1b. Leaves cauline . . . 6

2a. Single leaf present; stem leaves, if any, reduced to bracts . . . 3
2b. Two leaves present . . . 4

3a. Lip squared; spur thickened at base . . . **northern club-spur orchis,**
     P. clavellata var. *ophioglossoides*
3b. Lip triangular; spur tapered to base . . . **blunt-leaved rein orchis,**
     P. obtusata

4a. Lip triangular . . . **Hooker's orchis,** *P. hookeri*
4b. Lip oblong . . . 5

5a. Spur less than 28 mm long . . . **pad-leaved orchis,** *P. orbiculata*
5b. Spur greater than 28 mm long . . . **Goldie's pad-leaved orchis, or large**
     pad-leaved orchis, *P. macrophylla*

6a. Lip margin fringed . . . 7
6b. Lip margin entire . . . 15

7a. Lip divided into three parts . . . 8
7b. Lip entire . . . 11

8a. Flowers green or whitish green . . . **green fringed orchis, or ragged orchis,**
     P. lacera
8b. Flowers otherwise . . . 9

9a. Flowers creamy white . . . **eastern prairie fringed orchis,** *P. leucophaea*
9b. Flowers purple . . . 10

10a. Lip fringed to less than one-third its length; petals oval-elliptic; column
     opening a transverse oval; flowering later than *P. grandiflora* in eastern part
     of the range . . . **small purple fringed orchis,** *P. psycodes*
10b. Lip fringed to more than one-third its length; petals oblong, spatulate;
     column opening rounded; flowering earlier than *P. psycodes* in eastern
     portions of the range . . . **large purple fringed orchis,** *P. grandiflora*

11a. Flowers pure white . . . 12
11b. Flowers cream, orange, or yellow . . . 13

12a. Lip narrowed; spur greatly exceeding lip; plants of the coastal plain from
     Cape Cod southward along the coast . . . **southern white fringed orchis,**
     P. blephariglottis var. *conspicua*

12b. Lip broadened to apex; spur only somewhat exceeding lip; plant generally distributed . . . **northern white fringed orchis**, *P. blephariglottis* var. *blephariglottis*

13a. Spur exceeding the ovary . . . **orange (yellow) fringed orchis**, *P. ciliaris*
13b. Spur equal to or less than the ovary . . . 14

14a. Lip recurved, flowers pale cream; restricted to eastern Long Island . . . **pale fringed orchis**, *P. pallida*
14b. Lip projecting forward; flowers orange to yellow; plants of Bristol County, Massachusetts, and eastern Long Island . . . **orange (yellow) crested orchis**, *P. cristata*

15a. Lip broadest at summit . . . **little club-spur orchis**, *P. clavellata* var. *clavellata*
15b. Lip narrowed at summit . . . 16

16a. Lip broadest below the middle, tubercle present on lip . . . **northern tubercled orchis**, *P. flava* var. *herbiola*
16b. Lip narrowed from base to summit . . . 17

17a. Flowers white . . . **tall white northern bog orchis**, *P. dilatata*
17b. Flowers green or greenish . . . 18

18a. Lip dilated at base; flowers mint green to whitish green; usually densely flowered, with lip recurved at maturity . . . **green bog orchis**, *P. huronensis*
18b. Lip tapered to base; flowers green to yellow-green; usually loosely flowered, with lip descending at maturity . . . **northern green bog orchis**, *P. hyperborea*

Platanthera blephariglottis (Willdenow) Lindley var. *blephariglottis*

Northern White Fringed Orchis

New England, New York, Pennsylvania, New Jersey
Michigan to Newfoundland, south to Illinois; Ohio to New Jersey

  forma *holopetala* (Lindley) P.M. Brown: entire-lip form

bogs, damp meadows
June 28–August 25

height: 15–60 cm   flowers: 10–30, 1–1.5 cm
white

occasional throughout the region; inland

color photos 115–117

This large, showy member of the fringed-lipped section *Blephariglottis* is widespread throughout the Northeast and has been vouchered from nearly every county. It, like several other *Platanthera* species, responds to habitat succession and often flowers best a few years after nearby woody plants have been disturbed (by burning, hurricanes, mowing, etc.).

northern white fringed orchis

Platanthera blephariglottis (Willdenow) Lindley var. *conspicua* (Ames) Luer

Southern White Fringed Orchis

Massachusetts, Connecticut, Rhode Island, New York, New Jersey
southeastern Massachusetts to Florida, west to Texas

wet meadows, power lines, borrow pits, bogs
July 18–August 21

height: 20–60 cm   flowers: 8–60, 2.5–4 cm
white

rare to local along the coast

color photo 118

This variety replaces the typical variety from Cape Cod southward along the coast. The spur of var. *conspicua* is much longer and the plants are taller than var. *blephariglottis*. It was formerly thought to occur only as far north as southern New Jersey, but careful examination of the coastal plain plants revealed that var. *conspicua* does indeed grow farther north.

southern white fringed orchis

Platanthera ciliaris (Linnaeus) Lindley

Orange (Yellow) Fringed Orchis

(Massachusetts), Connecticut, Rhode Island, New York, Pennsylvania, New Jersey
Michigan to Massachusetts, south to Texas and Florida

wet thickets, damp meadows
July 20–September 5

height: 20–50 cm   flowers: 25–115, 1.5–3 cm
brilliant orange to yellow

rare to local in Connecticut, Rhode Island, New York, and adjacent Pennsylvania and New Jersey; historical in Massachusetts

color photos 119–121

The tall, brilliant orange plumes of this showy orchid are unmistakable in the August sun. Succession and loss of habitat have greatly reduced the number of sites for this species in the northeastern United States. Currently there are large populations in southern Rhode Island (discovered in August 1993), southern Connecticut, and eastern Long Island. The species was previously known from Massachusetts but has not been seen there in more than 25 years.

regionally significant species

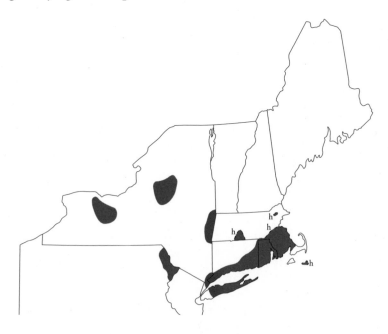

orange (yellow) fringed orchis

Platanthera clavellata (Michaux) Luer var. *clavellata*

Little Club-spur Orchis

New England, New York, Pennsylvania, New Jersey
Wisconsin to Maine, south to Georgia

bogs, meadows, wet woods, borrow pits, wet ditches
June 8–August 29

height: 10–20 cm   flowers: 12–30, 4–7 mm
green to straw yellow

occasional to frequent throughout the southern portions of the region; becoming rare northward

color photo 122

This is one of the smallest *Platanthera* species in the Northeast. The typical
variety is found primarily in wet woodlands throughout the southern counties
of New England, New York, and adjacent Pennsylvania and New Jersey.

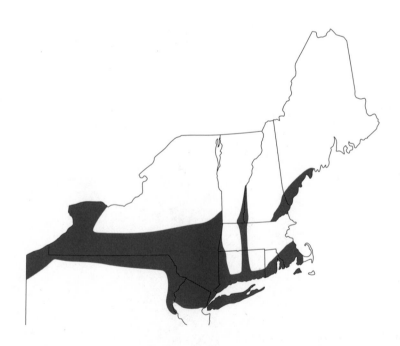

little club-spur orchis

Platanthera clavellata (Michaux) Luer
   var. *ophioglossoides* (Fernald) P.M. Brown

Northern Club-spur Orchis

New England, New York, Pennsylvania, New Jersey
Ontario to Newfoundland, south to Michigan and Massachusetts

bogs, meadows, wet woods, borrow pits, wet ditches
June 8–August 29

var. *ophioglossoides* plants are somewhat smaller and more compact than var.
   clavellata; a single leaf is present near the base of the stem

occasional to frequent in the northern portions of the region

color photo 123

The **northern club-spur orchis** grows primarily in open habitats, often in the
company of *P. blephariglottis* var. *blephariglottis*. It is easily separated from the
little club-spur orchis, var. *clavellata*, by its single large leaf and dense inflorescence of straw-colored flowers.

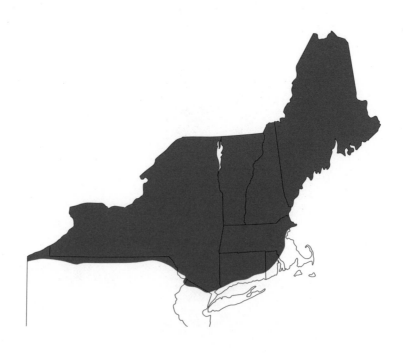

northern club-spur orchis

Platanthera cristata (Michaux) Lindley

Orange (Yellow) Crested Orchis

Massachusetts, New York
Massachusetts south to Florida and west to Texas

damp oak-pine woods, moist roadsides
July 25–August 15

height: 10–20 cm   flowers: 12–60, 4–7 mm
orange to yellow

color photos 124, 125

This species may at first glance appear to be a smaller edition of *P. ciliaris*, but the different petal structures of the two should be evident on closer examination. It is very rare and local in the Northeast; known only from a small population in Bristol County, Massachusetts, and eastern Long Island.

regionally significant species

orange (yellow) crested orchis

Platanthera dilatata (Pursh) Lindley var. *dilatata*

Tall White Northern Bog Orchis

Maine, New Hampshire, Vermont, Massachusetts, (Connecticut), New York, Pennsylvania

Alaska to Newfoundland, south to California and New Mexico, Minnesota and Indiana, and Pennsylvania

calcareous wet woods, bogs, and pond shores; often in roadside ditches in the north

June 10–September 5

height: 30–108 cm   flowers: 18–135, 0.75–1 cm
white; spicy fragrance

occasional to frequent in the north; rare to local southward

color photo 126

The delightful cinnamon-and-sugar fragrance of this statuesque summer orchid makes it a favorite among orchid enthusiasts. It is most at home in northern New England and New York, often in roadside ditches and open boggy meadows and swamps. Occasional disjunct sites occur in southern counties. Two other varieties are found in western North America.

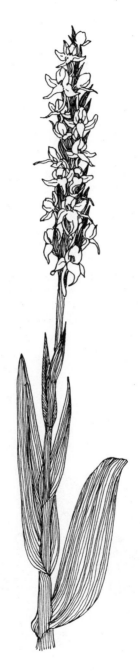

tall white northern bog orchis

Platanthera flava (Linnaeus) Lindley var. *herbiola* (R. Brown) Luer

Northern Tubercled Orchis

New England, New York, Pennsylvania, New Jersey
Minnesota to Nova Scotia, south to Missouri and Georgia, to the southern Appalachian Mountains

forma *lutea* (Boivin) Whiting & Catling: yellow-flowered form

wet meadows, banks, floodplains
June 12–August 15

height: 10–30 cm   flowers: 15–45, 4–7 mm
grass-green

rare to local throughout the region; becoming more frequent in southern areas

color photos 127–129

This obscure, grass-green, fragrant orchid was once considered one of the rarer orchids in the Northeast, but intensive field searches have revealed large, stable populations in several states. The species is by no means common or even frequent, and is still listed as Special Concern or Threatened in each state, but it is no longer a candidate for federal listing. The sweet, perfumelike fragrance is often detected before the actual plant. The variety *flava*, which occurs primarily in the southeastern and south-central United States, has a disjunct population in southwestern Nova Scotia.

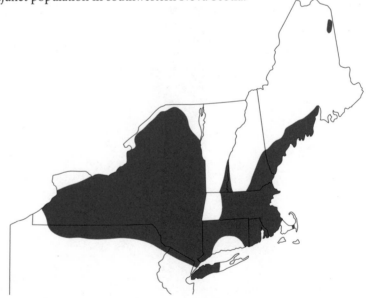

northern tubercled orchis

Platanthera grandiflora (Bigelow) Lindley

Large Purple Fringed Orchis

New England, New York, Pennsylvania, New Jersey
Minnesota to Newfoundland, south to West Virginia and New Jersey; south in the
Appalachian Mountains to Georgia

forma *albiflora* (Rand & Redfield) Catling: white-flowered form
forma *carnea* P.M. Brown: pink-flowered form
froma *mentotonsa* (Fernald) P.M. Brown: entire-lip form

wet woods, streamsides, meadows, thickets
June 14–August 12

height: 30–90 cm   flowers: 12–85, 1–2 cm
various shades of purple from pale lavender to rosy magenta

local to occasional throughout the Northeast; less common in or absent from
the immediate coastal plain

color photos 130–133

Widespread throughout the nine-state region, this tall (to 1 meter), stately
orchid is a summer feature, especially in northern New England. It usually
occurs in small numbers, often as a single plant, but every once in a while a
large stand of more than 100 plants is found. One site I observed in northern
New Hampshire in July 1993 had 134 flowering stems, many nearly 1 meter
tall.

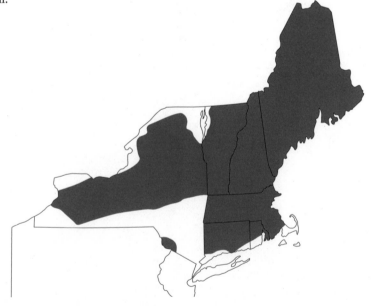

small purple fringed orchis

large purple fringed orchis

Platanthera hookeri (Torrey) Lindley

Hooker's Orchis

Maine, New Hampshire, Vermont, Massachusetts, (Connecticut), Rhode Island, New York, Pennsylvania, New Jersey
Manitoba to Newfoundland, south to Iowa and New Jersey

rich mesic forests
May 15–July 12

height: 13–34 cm   flowers: 4–12, 2–3 cm
green

local, perhaps declining, throughout the region; historical in Connecticut

color photos 134, 135

This has perhaps the most curious flowers of all our *Platanthera* species. The flowers have been described as resembling both ice tongs and a gargoyle. At any rate, on close examination the flowers never fail to pique curiosity among students. The species is uncommon to rare throughout the region.

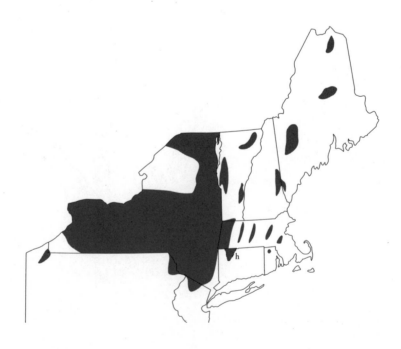

Hooker's orchis

Platanthera huronensis (Linnaeus) Lindley

Green Bog Orchis

New England, New York, Pennsylvania, New Jersey
Alaska to Newfoundland, south to California and Pennsylvania

swamps, bogs, and ditches
May 28–September 12

height: 15–75 cm   flowers: 12–170, 4–6 mm
pale green to chartreuse

occasional to frequent in northern areas; rare to local in southern regions

color photos 136, 137

This and the **northern green bog orchis**, *P. hyperborea*, are perhaps the two most easily confused of the green-flowered *Platanthera* species in the Northeast. They have been taxonomically merged and segregated over the years (see Synonyms for Currrent Nomenclature). The current view, that they are separate species, simply supports the original descriptions. *Platanthera huronensis* is the more frequent of the two and is widespread throughout northern and western counties in the region. It is usually absent from the coastal plain. Large stands often grow in wet roadside ditches and seeping hillsides, often with individuals 75 or more centimeters tall. Plants vary greatly in size and vigor and therefore the number of flowers per plant is quite variable.

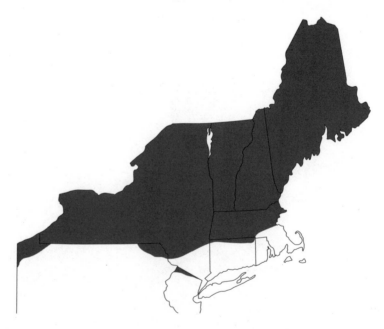

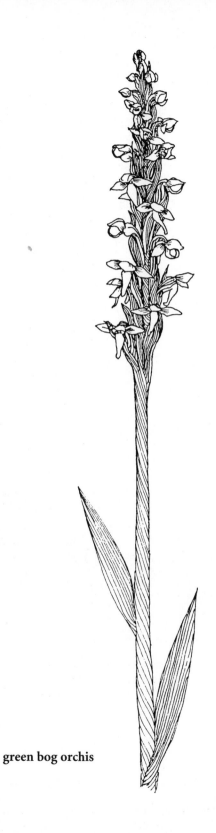

green bog orchis

Platanthera hyperborea (Linnaeus) Lindley var. *hyperborea*

Northern Green Bog Orchis

Maine, New Hampshire, Vermont, Massachusetts, New York
Alaska to Newfoundland, south to California, New Mexico, and Iowa, and east to
    Massachusetts

swamps, bogs, and ditches
June 18–August 24

height: 15–60 cm   flowers: 9–40+, 3–5 mm
lime green

rare to local in northern and western New England; rare in New York

color photos 138, 139

See the notes for *P. huronensis*. The distribution of this species is considerably
more limited. It occurs primarily in the far northern counties; in the Northeast
it shows a preference for calcareous soils. Its habitat is similar to that of *P.
huronensis*, although *P. hyperborea* plants are always smaller and have fewer
flowers. Three additional varieties occur in western North America.

northern green bog orchis

Platanthera lacera (Michaux) G. Don

Green Fringed Orchis, or Ragged Orchis

New England, New York, Pennsylvania, New Jersey
Manitoba to Newfoundland, south to Oklahoma and Georgia

damp fields, meadows, swamps
June 29–September 6

height: 20–60 cm   flowers: 12–45, 1.5–3 cm
shades of green, occasionally near white

occasional throughout the entire region; vouchered from every county

color photo 140

The least conspicuous of the fringed orchises, this species is also the most frequent. It can be found throughout the summer in damp meadows, open wet woods, and roadside ditches in all counties of New England, New York, and adjacent Pennsylvania and New Jersey.

green fringed orchis, or ragged orchis

Platanthera leucophaea (Nuttall) Lindley

Eastern Prairie Fringed Orchis

(Maine, New York)
Nebraska to Maine, south to Oklahoma and Virginia

fens, prairies
July 18–August 13

height: 30–85 cm   flowers: 5–20, 1.75–3 cm
creamy white

rare in southern Aroostook County, Maine, and central New York; plants
bloom at very sporadic intervals, which makes accurate assessment of their
status difficult

color photo 141

Although this species must be listed as historical in Maine and New York, the
only states in the Northeast where it has ever occurred, local botanists have
always been optimistic that it will bloom again in the near future. It is the habit
of this prairie species to rest for many years between bloomings, and it often
responds to burning. It is a plant of calcareous fens in the East and of the true
prairies in midwestern North America, the center of its population. The large,
fragrant, fringed flowers are among the most beautiful in the genus *Platanthera*.

Threatened

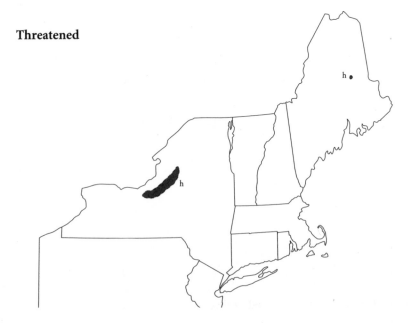

eastern prairie fringed orchis

Platanthera macrophylla (Goldie) P.M. Brown

Goldie's Pad-leaved Orchis, or Large Pad-leaved Orchis

Maine, New Hampshire, Vermont, Massachusetts, (Connecticut), Rhode Island, New York, Pennsylvania
Ontario to Newfoundland, south to Michigan and Pennsylvania

rich mesic forests
June 27–August 11

height: 30–75 cm   flowers: 6–30, 2–3 cm; spur to 28–40 mm
greenish white

local and scattered in northern areas; rare in southern regions

color photos 142, 143

This species and *P. orbiculata* are often confused with each other in the literature, but in my extensive fieldwork I have found them to be quite distinct. One population in east-central New Hampshire has several hundred plants of *P. macrophylla* and a few plants of *P. orbiculata*. Flower size, spur length, petal placement, and lip shape remain consistent within each species. Both species prefer rich mesic forests with little or no woody understory. **Goldie's pad-leaved orchis** grows in scattered spots throughout New England and New York and adjacent Pennsylvania, and is considered historical in Connecticut.

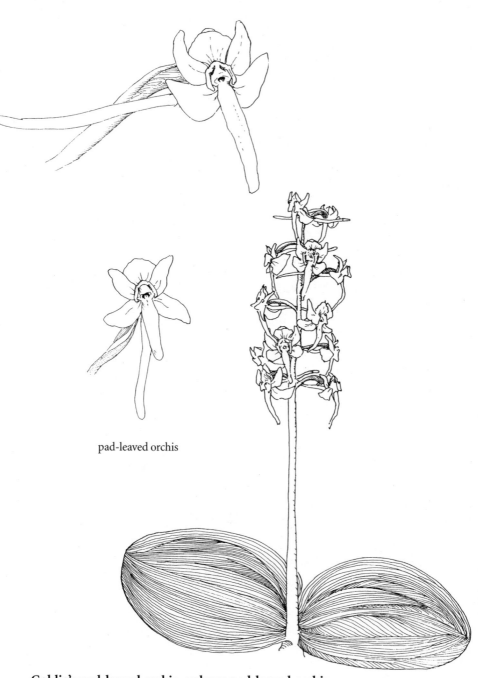

pad-leaved orchis

Goldie's pad-leaved orchis, or large pad-leaved orchis

Platanthera obtusata (Banks ex Pursh) Lindley

Blunt-leaved Rein Orchis

Maine, New Hampshire, Vermont, (Massachusetts), New York
Alaska to Newfoundland, south to Colorado, the Great Lakes, and western Massachusetts

   forma *foliosa* P.M. Brown: multiple-leaved form

northern white cedar swamps and thickets
June 18–August 26

height: 8–16 cm   flowers: 3–12, 4–7 mm
green

local in northern Maine, New Hampshire, Vermont, and New York; historical in Massachusetts

color photos 144–146

This little denizen of the cool northern forests and northern white cedar and spruce swamps is often overlooked because of its overall size (usually less than 12 cm), small greenish flowers, and single leaf. It is known only from the far northern counties and a historical disjunct record from western Massachusetts.

blunt-leaved rein orchis

Platanthera orbiculata (Pursh) Lindley

Pad-leaved Orchis

Maine, New Hampshire, Vermont, Massachusetts, (Connecticut), Rhode Island,
New York, Pennsylvania, New Jersey
British Columbia to Newfoundland, south to Washington and Maryland, south to
North Carolina in the Appalachian Mountains

usually rich mesic forests
June 23–August 20

height: 15–30 cm   flowers: 5–26, 1–1.5 cm; spur to 28 mm
watery green to white

local to occasional throughout the region; rare in New Jersey; historical in
Connecticut

color photos 147, 148

See comments for *P. macrophylla*.

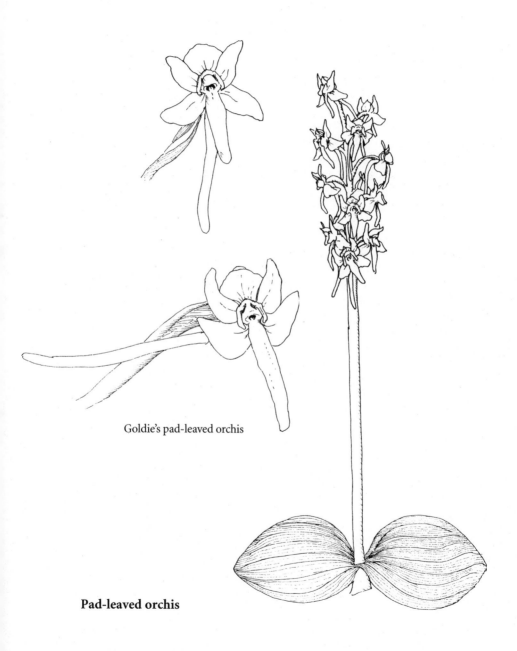

Goldie's pad-leaved orchis

Pad-leaved orchis

Platanthera pallida P.M. Brown

Pale Fringed Orchis

New York

dry interdunal hollows among pitch pines
July 25–August 19

height: 20–85 cm   flowers: 20–115, 3–5 mm
pale creamy ivory

rare; endemic to eastern Long Island

color photos 149, 150

This is the newest species of orchid to be documented from the Northeast. Its range is restricted to three sites in eastern Long Island, where it grows in dry interdunal hollows with pitch pine and scrub oak. The showy, pale creamy yellow flowers appear in late July and August. The plants were originally thought to be pale-flowered forms of *P. cristata*, but my research supports the conclusion that this is a separate species.

nationally significant species

pale fringed orchis

Platanthera psycodes (Linnaeus) Lindley

Small Purple Fringed Orchis

New England, New York, Pennsylvania, New Jersey
Minnesota to Newfoundland, south to Ohio and New Jersey, and to Georgia in the
Appalachian Mountains

forma *albiflora* (R. Hoffman) Whiting & Catling: white-flowered form
forma *ecalcarata* (Bryan) P.M. Brown: spurless form
forma *rosea* P.M. Brown: pink-flowered form
forma *varians* (Bryan) P.M. Brown: entire-lip form

damp meadows, streamsides, wet woods, swamps
July 15–September 19

height: 30–110 cm   flowers: 20–135, 5–10 mm
various shades of purple from pale lilac to rosy magenta

occasional throughout the region

color photos 151–154

The common names **large** and **small purple fringed orchis** are misleading as
the latter is often larger than the former—both taller and more floriferous—
although the individual flowers are smaller. This species often occupies the
same habitat as *P. grandiflora*, but in New England flowers later (August–
September).

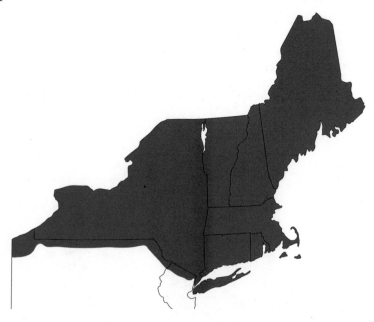

large purple fringed orchis

small purple fringed orchis

Platanthera Hybrids

Platanthera ×*andrewsii* (Niles) Luer
Andrews' Hybrid Fringed Orchis
(*P. lacera* × *P. psycodes*)
color photo 155

Platanthera ×*bicolor* (Rafinesque) Luer
Bicolor Hybrid Fringed Orchis
(*P. blephariglottis* var. *conspicua* × *P. ciliaris*)
color photo 156

Platanthera ×*canbyi* (Ames) Luer
Canby's Hybrid Fringed Orchis
(*P. blephariglottis* var. *conspicua* × *P. cristata*)
color photo 157

Platanthera ×*channellii* Folsom
Channell's Hybrid Fringed Orchis
(*P. ciliaris* × *P. cristata*)
color photo 158

Platanthera ×*keenanii* P.M. Brown
Keenan's Hybrid Fringed Orchis
(*P. grandiflora* × *P. lacera*)
color photo 159

Platanthera ×*media* (Rydberg) Luer
Intermediate Hybrid Rein Orchis
(*P. hyperborea* var. *hyperborea* × *P. dilatata* var. *dilatata*)
color photo 160

Platanthera ×*vossii* Case
Voss' Hybrid Rein Orchis
(*P. blephariglottis* var. *blephariglottis* × *P. clavellata* var. *ophioglossoides*)
color photo 161

P. grandiflora × *P. psycodes*
P. pallida × *P. blephariglottis* var. *conspicua*

Pogonia ophioglossoides (Linnaeus) Ker-Gawler var. *ophioglossoides*

Rose Pogonia

New England, New York, Pennsylvania, New Jersey
Ontario to Newfoundland, south to Texas and Florida

　　forma *albiflora* Rand & Redfield: white-flowered form

bogs, swamps, wet meadows, borrow pits
June 10–August 12

height: 10–25 cm　　flowers: 1–3 (rarely 4), 1.5–4.5 cm
rosy pink to lavender

occasional throughout the region; locally abundant

color photos 162–164

This is one of the most conspicuous pink orchids of our wet meadows, swales, and bogs. It often occurs in large numbers (10,000+), and plants may have as many as three, rarely four, flowers per stem, although one flower is typical. Known from all counties in New England, New York, and adjacent Pennsylvania and New Jersey. The variety *brachypogon* occurs only in Nova Scotia.

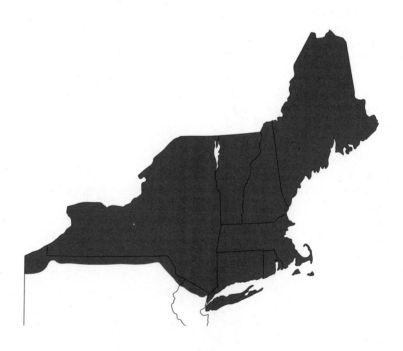

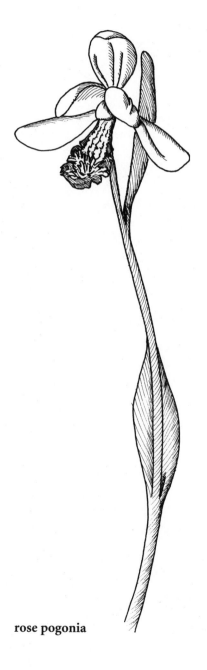

rose pogonia

Key to *Spiranthes* (Ladies'-tresses)

1a. Leaves narrow and grasslike at flowering time . . . 2
1b. Leaves orbicular, or absent at flowering time . . . 6

Spiranthes cernua, *ochroleuca*, and *casei* may flower without leaves present, especially later in the season and in drought years, but evidence of the narrow leaves is usually visible.

2a. Lip with bright yellow central portion . . . **shining ladies'-tresses**, *S. lucida*
2b. Lip otherwise . . . 3

3a. Flowers entirely white . . . 4
3b. Flowers otherwise . . . 8

4a. Lip panduriform (constricted) . . . **hooded ladies'-tresses**, *S. romanzoffiana*
4b. Lip oval to oblong . . . 5

5a. Flowers in a single rank; plants of wet areas in eastern Long Island . . . **giant ladies'-tresses**, *S. praecox*

Spiranthes praecox has raised green veins throughout the southern portion of its range; see notes for *S. praecox* for details.

5b. Flowers in multiple ranks; plants widespread in moist habitats, with a variety of morphologies . . . **nodding ladies'-tresses**, *S. cernua*

6a. Flowers with a green central portion . . . 7
6b. Flowers without a green central portion . . . **little ladies'-tresses**, *S. tuberosa*

7a. Flowers loosely arranged on the spike, spike with few if any twists, these usually near the summit; basal leaves often present at flowering time . . . **northern slender ladies'-tresses**, *S. lacera* var. *lacera*
7b. Flowers densely arranged on spike, spike regularly twisted; basal leaves rarely present at flowering time . . . **southern slender ladies'-tresses**, *S. lacera* var. *gracilis*

8a. Flowers yellowish to white, underside of lip yellow . . . **yellow ladies'-tresses**, *S. ochroleuca*
8b. Flowers white with yellow to beige lip . . . 9

9a. Flowers slender, never fully expanded; plants of northern areas . . . **Case's ladies'-tresses**, *S. casei*
9b. Flowers fully expanded, lip color contrasts with color of petals and sepals . . . **grass-leaved ladies'-tresses**, *S. vernalis*

Spiranthes casei Catling & Cruise var. *casei*

Case's Ladies'-tresses

Maine, New Hampshire, Vermont, New York, Pennsylvania
Ontario to Nova Scotia, south to Michigan, Pennsylvania, and Maine

dry, shaley roadsides, thin-soil fields
August 25–September 15

height: 15–35 cm   flowers: 8–35, 4–6 mm
petals creamy white; lip pale yellow

rare and local in northern Maine, New Hampshire, Vermont, and New York

color photos 165, 166

Recently described as a new species, this inhabitant of northernmost New Hampshire, northern Vermont, and western Maine is restricted to the shale banks and thin-soil habitats of the Canadian Shield and barely comes southward into New England. In September 1996 extensive fieldwork revealed small colonies of *S. casei* in a number of additional roadsides in northern Vermont extending as far west as Hardwick. It has been found in similar habitats in northern New York, and although an extensive colony of more than 1000 plants near Speculator, New York, was destroyed by roadwork, additional extensive colonies were found in 1996 along New York State Route 10 southwest of Speculator. Extant sites also exist in the Pennsylvania counties that border central New York. This species was known for some time as the "northern *vernalis*" and even in Carlyle Luer's monumental work is identified (incorrectly) as *S. intermedia*. The variety *novaescotiae* occurs only in southern Nova Scotia.

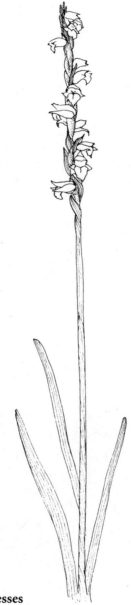

Case's ladies'-tresses

Spiranthes cernua (Linnaeus) L.C. Richard

Nodding Ladies'-tresses

New England, New York, Pennsylvania, New Jersey
South Dakota to Nova Scotia, south to Texas and Florida

damp roadsides, disturbed areas, meadows, ditches
August 25–November 8

height: 6–52 cm   flowers: 10–60, 0.5–1.5 cm
white

occasional to frequent throughout the region

color photos 167–169, 178

If you were to count the individual stems of the orchids in the Northeast, this species most likely would be the winner. It occurs in all counties in the nine-state region, usually in roadside ditches, damp meadows, and disturbed wetlands. This species is highly variable in form and occurs in at least three habitat-related morphologies. The most distinct of these is the robust coastal form, which ranges from southwestern Nova Scotia and Goose Rocks Beach, Maine, southward beyond our limits. It is an impressive plant, often 30 cm or more tall, with very large (1–1.5 cm) flowers that have a square or blocky appearance.

nodding ladies'-tresses

Spiranthes lacera Rafinesque var. *lacera*

Northern Slender Ladies'-tresses

New England, New York, Pennsylvania
Manitoba to Nova Scotia, south to Missouri and Virginia

dry, thin, open woods; exposed bluffs; roadcuts; and gravelly roadsides
July 10–August 25

height: 10–25 cm   flowers: 8–20, 2–4 mm
white with a green throat
leaves often present at flowering time

occasional in northern areas; becoming local in southern counties, and absent
    from the coastal plain

color photos 170, 171

See the comments for *S. lacera* var. *gracilis*. The variety *lacera* is confined to
the more northerly counties in the region; where the two varieties overlap they
are clearly differentiated by their morphological characteristics.

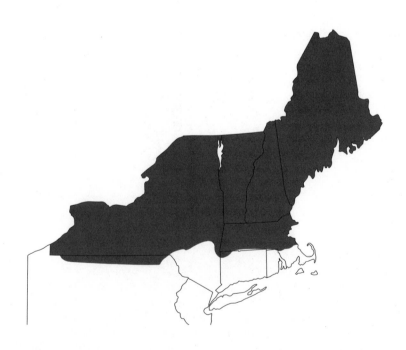

northern slender ladies'-tresses

Spiranthes lacera Rafinesque var. *gracilis* (Bigelow) Luer

Southern Slender Ladies'-tresses

New England, New York, Pennsylvania, New Jersey
Kansas, north to Michigan and Maine, south to Texas and Florida

dry to damp grasslands; thin, open woods
July 10–September 8

height: 13–30 cm   flowers: 12–40, 3–5 mm
white with a green throat
leaves often absent at flowering time

occasional throughout the southern region, becoming rare northward; often
    absent from the northern counties

color photos 172, 173

This variety and *S. lacera* var. *lacera* are sometimes considered separate species. Even though they are quite distinct in the Northeast and are easily identified as separate taxa, I follow the recent nomenclature of Paul Catling and
Charles Sheviak and treat them as varieties of a single species. *Spiranthes
lacera* var. *gracilis* is the more southerly of the two and grows in nearly every
county in southern and central New England, New York, and adjacent Pennsylvania and New Jersey. It blooms in midsummer in dry to damp grasslands,
meadows, and roadsides.

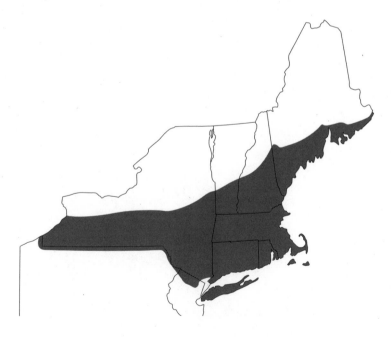

southern slender ladies'-tresses

Spiranthes lucida (H.H. Eaton) Ames

Shining Ladies'-tresses

Maine, New Hampshire, Vermont, Massachusetts, Connecticut, (Rhode Island),
  New York, Pennsylvania, New Jersey
Wisconsin to Nova Scotia, south to Kansas and West Virginia

limy pond shores, riverbanks, meadows, road banks, and seeps
May 25–July 19

height: 5–15 cm   flowers: 5–18, 5–10 mm
white with a bright yellow lip and throat

rare to local throughout the Northeast; historical in Rhode Island

color photos 174, 175

This is our only late spring–blooming *Spiranthes* and the only one whose lip
has a bright yellow center. It prefers calcareous seeps and meadows, and
therefore is confined to geographic areas with such habitats, primarily western
New England, northern New York, and northern Maine. Disjunct sites have
occurred or do occur elsewhere where lime deposits reach the surface. It is
known from all nine states.

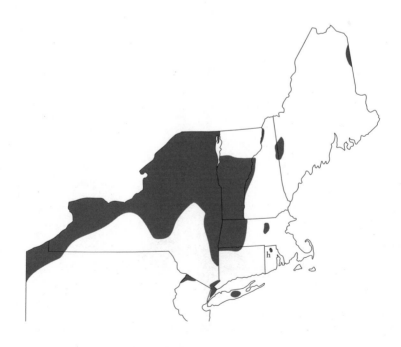

shining ladies'-tresses

Spiranthes ochroleuca (Rydberg) Rydberg

Yellow Ladies'-tresses

New England, New York, Pennsylvania, New Jersey
Michigan to Nova Scotia, south to Kentucky and Virginia

dry to damp roadsides, thin woods, borrow pits, and disturbed areas; prefers
    drier areas
August 20–October 28

height: 8–20 cm   flowers: 12–35, 5–8 mm
creamy white with a butterscotch-colored throat

occasional throughout the region; rare and local in the far northern counties
    of New England

color photos 176–178

Restored to its rightful taxonomic rank through the efforts of Charles Sheviak
and Paul Catling, this species is often found growing in company with *S.
cernua*, the latter occupying the wet lower portions of the slopes and banks
and *S. ochroleuca* on the drier upper portions. In the Willoughby Lake region
of northeastern Vermont you can find roadside banks with five *Spiranthes*
species in appropriate habitats on the same bank: *S. lacera, casei*, and
ochroleuca on the upper portions; *S. cernua* and *romanzoffiana* in the lower,
wetter areas.

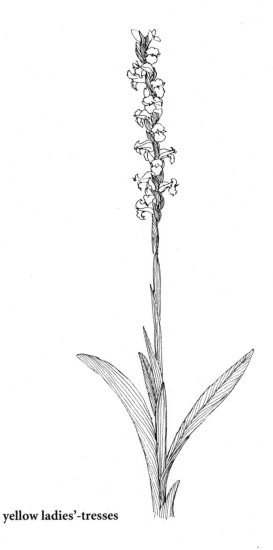

yellow ladies'-tresses

Spiranthes praecox (Walter) S. Watson forma *albolabia* Brown & McCartney

Giant Ladies'-tresses

New York
New York south to Florida and west to Texas

> forma *albolabia* Brown & McCartney: white-lipped form

swampy woods (in the north)
September 15–October 25

height: 30–45 cm   flowers: 13–54, 5–10 mm
white; in the southern part of the range the raised veins of the lip are green, but
northern plants have white lips

rare; known from a single locality in eastern Long Island

color photo 179

The presence of *S. praecox* in eastern Long Island (and coastal New Jersey) presents an interesting problem in distribution. *Spiranthes praecox* occurs throughout the Deep South and northward along the Atlantic seaboard to southern Delaware. The southern plants are typical *S. praecox*: they are relatively early blooming and, more significant, they have the characteristic raised green veins on the lip (a few plants have yellow raised veins). The northern plants, forma *albolabia*, have entirely white lips but do possess the raised veins and general appearance of *S. praecox*; however, they bloom in late September–October. Pending further research these northern populations will remain *S. praecox*.

regionally significant species

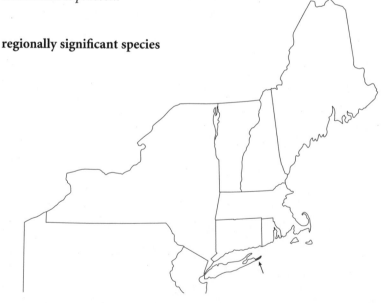

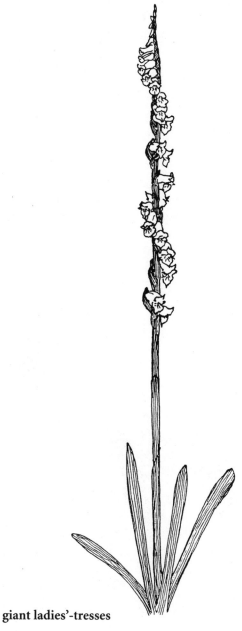

giant ladies'-tresses

Spiranthes romanzoffiana Chamisso

Hooded Ladies'-tresses

Maine, New Hampshire, Vermont, Massachusetts, New York, Pennsylvania
Alaska to Newfoundland, south to California and northern New Mexico, north to
    Idaho, and east to Pennsylvania

limy bogs, roadside ditches, riverbanks and cobbles, seeps
July 18–September 16

height: 10–25 cm   flowers: 12–45, 5–10 mm
white

rare to local in southern Maine, Vermont, New Hampshire, and central Mas-
    sachusetts; more frequent northward in calcareous areas

color photos 180, 181

This late summer–blooming species is found primarily in northern New England in rich calcareous bogs and seeps, often accompanied by **grass-of-
parnassus**, *Parnassia glauca* Rafinesque, and **Kalm's lobelia**, *Lobelia kalmii*
Linnaeus. It is known from northern Maine, New Hampshire (rare), Vermont, Massachusetts (rare), and northern New York.

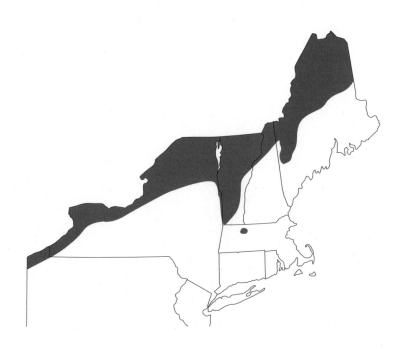

hooded ladies'-tresses

Spiranthes tuberosa Rafinesque

Little Ladies'-tresses

Massachusetts, (Connecticut), Rhode Island, New York
Michigan to Massachusetts, south to Texas and Florida

dry fields, cemeteries, roadsides
August 5–September 12

height: 8–15 cm   flowers: 8–20, 3–5 mm
pure white

rare to local in Massachusetts, Rhode Island, and Long Island; historical in
    Connecticut

color photo 182

This is the smallest of our ladies'-tresses. It is restricted to the southern coastal
plain and is presently known from southeastern Massachusetts, Rhode Island,
and Long Island. Dry, sunny grasslands are the preferred habitat.

regionally significant species

little ladies'-tresses

Spiranthes vernalis Engler & Gray

Grass-leaved Ladies'-tresses

New Hampshire, Massachusetts, Connecticut, Rhode Island, New York
New Hampshire south to Texas and Florida; Mexico

dry grassy fields and roadsides, cemeteries
July 20–September 10

height: 15–45 (60) cm   flowers: 12–38, 5–10 mm
creamy white with a darker lip

rare and local throughout its northern range

color photos 183, 184

The largest (to 60 cm) of the genus in our region, *S. vernalis* blooms in mid-summer on coastal plain grasslands. Roadsides and cemeteries are both excellent places to search for it. There are a few disjunct sites, in similar habitat, in southern New Hampshire and central Massachusetts, but this wild orchid is primarily found along the coast from Cape Cod to Long Island and southward.

regionally significant species

grass-leaved ladies'-tresses

65. Showy orchis, white-flowered form
Galearis spectabilis forma *gordinierii*

66. Showy orchis, pink-flowered form
Galearis spectabilis forma *willeyi*

67. Giant rattlesnake orchis
Goodyera oblongifolia

68. Giant rattlesnake orchis
Goodyera oblongifolia

An asterisk (∗) indicates that the species is introduced.

69. Giant rattlesnake orchis,
rosette of typical leaves
Goodyera oblongifolia

70. Giant rattlesnake orchis, reticulated-leaf form
Goodyera oblongifolia forma *reticulata*

71. Downy rattlesnake orchis
Goodyera pubescens

72. Downy rattlesnake orchis
Goodyera pubescens

74. Lesser rattlesnake orchis, white-veined-leaf form
Goodyera repens forma *ophioides*

73. Downy rattlesnake orchis
Goodyera pubescens

75. Lesser rattlesnake orchis,
white-veined-leaf form
Goodyera repens forma *ophioides*

76. Checkered rattlesnake orchis
Goodyera tesselata

78. *Goodyera pubescens* × *G. tesselata*

77. *Goodyera pubescens* × *G. tesselata*

79. Fragrant orchis*
Gymnadenia conopsea

80. Small whorled pogonia, flowering plant
with previous year's fruit
Isotria medeoloides

82. Small whorled pogonia, fruit
Isotria medeoloides

81. Small whorled pogonia
Isotria medeoloides

83. Large whorled pogonia
Isotria verticillata

84. Large whorled pogonia
Isotria verticillata

85. An unusual colony of large whorled pogonias after a fire, with no stems, just the flowers sitting on the ground
Isotria verticillata

86. Large whorled pogonia, flowering plant with previous year's fruit
Isotria verticillata

87. Lily-leaved twayblade
Liparis liliifolia

88. Lily-leaved twayblade
Liparis liliifolia

89. Lily-leaved twayblade, green-flowered form
Liparis liliifolia forma *viridiflora*

90. Loesel's twayblade
Liparis loeselii

92. Auricled twayblade
Listera auriculata

91. Loesel's twayblade
Liparis loeselii

93. Auricled twayblade
Listera auriculata

94. Southern twayblade
Listera australis

95. Southern twayblade
Listera australis

96. Broad-lipped twayblade
Listera convallarioides

97. Broad-lipped twayblade
Listera convallarioides

98. Broad-lipped twayblade, three-leaved form
Listera convallarioides forma *trifolia*

99. Heart-leaved twayblade, typical color
form (left) and forma *viridens*
Listera cordata var. *cordata*

100. Heart-leaved twayblade,
typical color form
Listera cordata var. *cordata*

101. Heart-leaved twayblade,
typical color form
Listera cordata var. *cordata*

102. Heart-leaved twayblade,
alternate-leaved form
Listera cordata var. *cordata* forma *disjuncta*

103. Heart-leaved twayblade,
three-leaved form
Listera cordata var. *cordata* forma *trifolia*

104. Heart-leaved twayblade,
variegated-leaf form
Listera cordata var. *cordata* forma *variegata*

106. Veltman's hybrid twayblade
Listera ×veltmanii

105. Small's twayblade
Listera smallii

107. Bayard's adder's-mouth
Malaxis bayardii

108. Bayard's adder's-mouth
Malaxis bayardii

109. White adder's-mouth
Malaxis brachypoda

110. White adder's-mouth
Malaxis brachypoda

111. White adder's-mouth, two-leaved form
Malaxis brachypoda forma *bifolia*

112. Green adder's-mouth
Malaxis unifolia

113. Green adder's-mouth
Malaxis unifolia

114. Green adder's-mouth, two-leaved form
Malaxis unifolia forma *bifolia*

115. Northern white fringed orchis
Platanthera blephariglottis var. *blephariglottis*

116. Northern white fringed orchis
Platanthera blephariglottis var. *blephariglottis*

117. Northern white fringed orchis, entire-lip form
Platanthera blephariglottis var. *blephariglottis* forma *holopetala*

118. Southern white fringed orchis
Platanthera blephariglottis var. *conspicua*

119. Orange fringed orchis
Platanthera ciliaris

120. Orange fringed orchis
Platanthera ciliaris

121. Orange fringed orchis
Platanthera ciliaris

122. Little club-spur orchis
Platanthera clavellata var. *clavellata*

123. Northern club-spur orchis
Platanthera clavellata var. *ophioglossoides*

124. Orange crested orchis
Platanthera cristata

125. Orange crested orchis
Platanthera cristata

126. Tall white northern bog orchis
Platanthera dilatata var. *dilatata*

127. Northern tubercled orchis
Platanthera flava var. *herbiola*

128. Northern tubercled orchis
Platanthera flava var. *herbiola*

Spiranthes Hybrids

Spiranthes ×*borealis* P.M. Brown

Northern Hybrid Ladies'-tresses
(*S. casei* × *S. ochroleuca*)
color photo 185

Spiranthes ×*intermedia* Ames
Intermediate Hybrid Ladies'-tresses
(*S. lacera* var. *gracilis* × *S. vernalis*)
color photo 186

Spiranthes ×*simpsonii* Catling & Sheviak
Simpson's Hybrid Ladies'-tresses
(*S. lacera* var. *lacera* × *S. romanzoffiana*)

S. casei × *S. romanzoffiana*
S. ochroleuca × *S. romanzoffiana*
S. cernua × *S. ochroleuca*
S. tuberosa × *S. lacera* var. *gracilis*
S. vernalis × *S. ochroleuca*
S. vernalis × *S. tuberosa*

Tipularia discolor (Pursh) Nuttall

Crane-fly Orchis

Massachusetts, New York
Michigan to Massachusetts, south to Texas and Florida

oak-holly-beech woodlands
July 25–August 15

height: 20–45 cm   flowers: 6–23, 2–3 cm
purple-brown

rare and local in Massachusetts and New York

color photos 187–189

In our area the **crane-fly orchis** is at the extreme northern limit of its range. It is currently known only from scattered populations on Martha's Vineyard and a large, vigorous site on eastern Long Island. There was formerly a very small population in mainland Massachusetts, but that was destroyed by housing construction. It prefers mixed forests of American beech, oak, and American holly, and flowers in midsummer.

regionally significant species

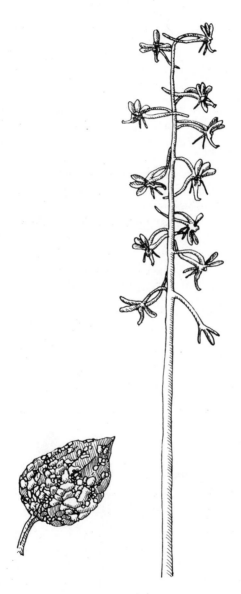

crane-fly orchis

Triphora trianthophora (Swartz) Rydberg var. *trianthophora*

Three Birds Orchis, or Nodding Pogonia

Maine, New Hampshire, Vermont, Massachusetts, (Connecticut), New York, New
    Jersey
Nebraska to Maine, south to Texas and Florida

forma *albidoflava* Keenan: white-flowered form

beech-hemlock forests
July 29–September 8

height: 3–7 cm   flowers: 1–4, 1.5 –2 cm
pink to white

local in New Hampshire; rare in Maine, Massachusetts, Vermont, New York,
    and New Jersey; historical in Connecticut

color photos 190–192

This is perhaps the most elusive orchid in the Northeast. The difficulty of
finding plants in bloom is complicated by the fact that the plants emerge only
one or two days before blooming, usually in mid-August. They often grow in
large colonies under American beech and, in the north, Canadian hemlock.
The colonies vary greatly from year to year in their thriftiness. In 1992 Philip
Keenan described an albino form, forma *albidoflava*, which is pure white and
has the green on the lip replaced by pale golden yellow. The variety *mexicana*
does not occur in the United States.

three birds orchis, or nodding pogonia

The scientific names of most organisms undergo significant revisions as time passes. Orchids are no exception. Most of the wild orchids of the Northeast have had nomenclatural revisions. There are two primary reasons a name is changed. Either new research reveals that a species has the characteristics of a different taxonomic grouping, or a name is determined to be invalid according to the rules of the International Code of Botanical Nomenclature.

The scientific name is a binomial: it comprises two parts, the genus name and the specific epithet. Both parts are written in Latin and italicized. The scientific name also includes the name of the author credited with describing the species—for example, *Orchis cristata* Michaux. Michaux was the first to publish a formal description of this orchid. Later, Lindley reclassified *Orchis cristata* to the genus *Platanthera*, retaining the epithet *cristata*. The orchid's scientific name became *Platanthera cristata* (Michaux) Lindley. Michaux's name was placed in parentheses to indicate that he was the original author, and Lindley's name was added to show that he transferred the species to the genus *Platanthera*.

Another author, R. Brown, also transferred *Orchis cristata* to a different genus, this time to *Habenaria*. He named the species *Habenaria cristata* (Michaux) R. Brown. But this name is not considered valid. So, although the name *Habenaria cristata* (Michaux) R. Brown has appeared in records and the literature, it is treated as a synonym of *Platanthera cristata* (Michaux) Lindley.

The dates of orchid name changes and the corresponding literature citations can be found in such large technical works as Correll's *Native Orchids of North America* and Luer's two-volume *Native Orchids of the United States and Canada*.

Throughout this field guide I have used what I believe to be the correct, current nomenclature. For those species that can be taxonomically confusing, I have included the following list of synonyms.

Amerorchis rotundifolia (Banks ex Pursh) Hultén
small round-leaved orchis
syn. *Orchis rotundifolia* Banks ex Pursh

Calopogon tuberosus (Linnaeus) Britton, Sterns & Poggenberg
grass-pink
syn. *Calopogon pulchellus* (Salisbury) R. Brown

Coeloglossum viride (Linnaeus) Hartman var. *virescens* (Muhlenberg) Luer
long bracted green orchis
syn. *Habenaria viridis* (Linnaeus) R. Brown
    var. *bracteata* (Muhlenberg ex Willdenow) A. Gray

Cypripedium parviflorum Salisbury var. *parviflorum*
southern small yellow lady's-slipper
syn. *Cypripedium calceolus* var. *parviflorum* (Salisbury) Fernald in part

Cypripedium parviflorum Salisbury var. *makasin* (Farwell) Sheviak
northern small yellow lady's-slipper
syn. *Cypripedium calceolus* var. *parviflorum* (Salisbury) Fernald in part
syn. *Cypripedium parviflorum* Salisbury in part

Cypripedium parviflorum Salisbury var. *pubescens* (Willdenow) Knight
large yellow lady's-slipper
syn. *Cypripedium calceolus* var. *pubescens* (Willdenow) Correll
syn. *Cypripedium pubescens* Willdenow

Galearis spectabilis (Linnaeus) Rafinesque
showy orchis
syn. *Orchis spectabilis* Linnaeus

Goodyera oblongifolia forma *reticulata* (Boivin) P.M. Brown
giant rattlesnake orchis, reticulated form
syn. *Goodyera oblongifolia* var. *reticulata* Boivin

Goodyera repens forma *ophioides* (Fernald) P.M. Brown
lesser rattlesnake orchis, reticulated form
syn. *Goodyera repens* var. *ophioides* Fernald

Malaxis brachypoda (Gray) Fernald
white adder's-mouth
syn. *Malaxis monophyllos* (Linnaeus) Swartz
    var. *brachypoda* (A. Gray) Morris & Eames

Platanthera blephariglottis (Willdenow) Lindley
white fringed orchis
syn. *Habenaria blephariglottis* (Willdenow) Hooker

129. Northern tubercled orchis, yellow-flowered form
Platanthera flava var. *herbiola* forma *lutea*

130. Large purple fringed orchis
Platanthera grandiflora

131. Large purple fringed orchis,
white-flowered form
Platanthera grandiflora forma *albiflora*

132. Large purple fringed orchis,
pink-flowered form
Platanthera grandiflora forma *carnea*

133. Large purple fringed orchis, entire-lip form
Platanthera grandiflora forma *mentotonsa*

134. Hooker's orchis
Platanthera hookeri

135. Hooker's orchis
Platanthera hookeri

136. Green bog orchis
Platanthera huronensis

137. Green bog orchis
Platanthera huronensis

138. Northern green bog orchis
Platanthera hyperborea var. *hyperborea*

139. Northern green bog orchis
Platanthera hyperborea var. *hyperborea*

140. Green fringed orchis
Platanthera lacera

141. Eastern prairie fringed orchis
Platanthera leucophaea

142. Goldie's pad-leaved orchis
Platanthera macrophylla

143. Goldie's pad-leaved orchis
Platanthera macrophylla

144. Blunt-leaved rein orchis
Platanthera obtusata

145. Blunt-leaved rein orchis
Platanthera obtusata

146. Blunt-leaved rein orchis,
multiple-leaved form
Platanthera obtusata forma *foliosa*

147. Pad-leaved orchis
Platanthera orbiculata

148. Pad-leaved orchis
Platanthera orbiculata

149. Pale fringed orchis
Platanthera pallida

150. Pale fringed orchis
Platanthera pallida

151. Small purple fringed orchis
Platanthera psycodes

152. Small purple fringed orchis,
white-flowered form
Platanthera psycodes forma *albiflora*

153. Small purple fringed orchis,
pink-flowered form
Platanthera psycodes forma *rosea*

154. Small purple fringed orchis,
entire-lip form
Platanthera psycodes forma *varians*

155. Andrews' hybrid fringed orchis
Platanthera ×andrewsii

156. Bicolor hybrid fringed orchis
Platanthera ×bicolor

157. Canby's hybrid fringed orchis
Platanthera ×canbyi

158. Channell's hybrid fringed orchis
Platanthera ×channellii

159. Keenan's hybrid fringed orchis
Platanthera ×keenanii

160. Intermediate hybrid rein orchis
Platanthera ×media

Dick Sooy

162. Rose pogonia
Pogonia ophioglossoides var. *ophioglossoides*

161. Voss' hybrid rein orchis
Platanthera ×*vossii*

163. Rose pogonia
Pogonia ophioglossoides var. *ophioglossoides*

164. Rose pogonia, white-flowered form
Pogonia ophioglossoides var. *ophioglossoides*
forma *albiflora*

165. Case's ladies'-tresses
Spiranthes casei var. *casei*

166. Case's ladies'-tresses
Spiranthes casei var. *casei*

167. Nodding ladies'-tresses
Spiranthes cernua

168. Nodding ladies'-tresses
Spiranthes cernua

169. Nodding ladies'-tresses
Spiranthes cernua

170. Northern slender ladies'-tresses
Spiranthes lacera var. *lacera*

171. Northern slender ladies'-tresses
Spiranthes lacera var. *lacera*

172. Southern slender ladies'-tresses
Spiranthes lacera var. *gracilis*

173. Southern slender ladies'-tresses
Spiranthes lacera var. *gracilis*

174. Shining ladies'-tresses
Spiranthes lucida

175. Shining ladies'-tresses
Spiranthes lucida

176. Yellow ladies'-tresses
Spiranthes ochroleuca

177. Yellow ladies'-tresses
Spiranthes ochroleuca

178. Nodding ladies'-tresses (left)
and yellow ladies'-tresses
Spiranthes cernua and *S. ochroleuca*

179. Giant ladies'-tresses, white-lipped form
Spiranthes praecox forma *albolabia*

180. Hooded ladies'-tresses
Spiranthes romanzoffiana

181. Hooded ladies'-tresses
Spiranthes romanzoffiana

182. Little ladies'-tresses
Spiranthes tuberosa

183. Grass-leaved ladies'-tresses
Spiranthes vernalis

184. Grass-leaved ladies'-tresses
Spiranthes vernalis

185. Northern hybrid ladies'-tresses
Spiranthes ×borealis

186. Intermediate hybrid ladies'-tresses
Spiranthes ×intermedia

187. Crane-fly orchis
Tipularia discolor

188. Crane-fly orchis
Tipularia discolor

189. Crane-fly orchis, leaves
Tipularia discolor

190. Three birds orchis
Triphora trianthophora var. *trianthophora*

191. Three birds orchis
Triphora trianthophora var. *trianthophora*

192. Three birds orchis, white-flowered form
Triphora trianthophora var. *trianthophora*
forma *albidoflava*

Philip E. Keenan

Platanthera ciliaris (Linnaeus) Lindley
orange (yellow) fringed orchis
syn. *Habenaria ciliaris* (Linnaeus) R. Brown

Platanthera clavellata (Michaux) Luer var. **clavellata**
little club-spur orchis
syn. *Habenaria clavellata* (Michaux) Sprengel

Platanthera clavellata (Michaux) Luer
var. **ophioglossoides** (Fernald) P.M. Brown
northern club-spur orchis
syn. *Habenaria clavellata* (Michaux) Sprengel var. *ophioglossoides* Fernald

Platanthera cristata (Michaux) Lindley
orange (yellow) crested orchis
syn. *Habenaria cristata* (Michaux) R. Brown

Platanthera dilatata (Pursh) Lindley var. **dilatata**
tall white northern bog orchis
syn. *Habenaria dilatata* (Pursh) Hooker

Platanthera flava (Linnaeus) Lindley var. **herbiola** (R. Brown) Luer
northern tubercled orchis
syn. *Habenaria flava* (Linnaeus) Lindley var. *herbiola* (R. Brown) Ames & Correll

Platanthera grandiflora (Bigelow) Lindley
large purple fringed orchis
syn. *Habenaria fimbriata* (Dryander) R. Brown
syn. *Habenaria psycodes* (Linnaeus) Lindley var. *grandiflora* (Bigelow) A. Gray

Platanthera hookeri (Torrey) Lindley
Hooker's orchis
syn. *Habenaria hookeri* Torrey ex A. Gray

Platanthera huronensis (Linnaeus) Lindley
green bog orchis
syn. *Habenaria huronensis* (Nuttall) Sprengel
syn. *Habenaria hyperborea* (Linnaeus) R. Brown var. *huronensis* (Nuttall) Farwell
syn. *Platanthera hyperborea* (Linnaeus) Lindley var. *huronensis* (Nuttall) Luer

Platanthera hyperborea (Linnaeus) Lindley var. **hyperborea**
northern green bog orchis
syn. *Habenaria hyperborea* (Linnaeus) R. Brown var. **hyperborea**

Platanthera lacera (Michaux) G. Don
green fringed orchis, or ragged orchis
syn. *Habenaria lacera* (Michaux) Loddiges

Platanthera leucophaea (Nuttall) Lindley
eastern prairie fringed orchis
syn. *Habenaria leucophaea* (Nuttall) A. Gray

Platanthera macrophylla (Goldie) P.M. Brown
Goldie's pad-leaved orchis
syn. *Habenaria macrophylla* Goldie
syn. *Habenaria orbiculata* (Pursh) Lindley forma *macrophylla* (Goldie) F. Morris
syn. *Platanthera orbiculata* (Pursh) Lindley var. *macrophylla* (Goldie) Luer

Platanthera obtusata (Banks ex Pursh) Lindley
blunt-leaved rein orchis
syn. *Habenaria obtusata* (Banks ex Pursh) Richards

Platanthera orbiculata (Pursh) Lindley
pad-leaved orchis
syn. *Habenaria orbiculata* (Pursh) Torrey

Platanthera psycodes (Linnaeus) Lindley
small purple fringed orchis
syn. *Habenaria psycodes* (Linnaeus) Sprengel

Spiranthes lacera (Rafinesque) Rafinesque var. *gracilis* (Bigelow) Luer
southern slender ladies'-tresses
syn. *Spiranthes gracilis* (Bigelow) Beck

Spiranthes ochroleuca (Rydberg) Rydberg
yellow ladies'-tresses
syn. *Spiranthes cernua* (Linnaeus) L.C. Richard var. *ochroleuca* (Rydberg) Ames

Spiranthes tuberosa Rafinesque
little ladies'-tresses
syn. *Spiranthes grayi* var. *tuberosa* (Ames) Fernald
syn. *Spiranthes beckii* of authors

SELECTED BIBLIOGRAPHY

This selection includes recent publications with current taxonomic information as well as older works with classic treatments of native orchids.

Brackley, F.E. 1985. The orchids of New Hampshire. *Rhodora* 87:1–117.

Brown, P.M. 1988. Stalking the wild orchids: Checklist of New England orchids. *Wild Flower Notes* 3(1):4–29.

Brown, P.M. 1993. *A field and study guide to the orchids of New England and New York.* Orchis Press, Jamaica Plain, Mass.

Brown, P.M. 1995. *Checklist of the orchids of North America north of Mexico.* Special Publication 1. *North American Native Orchid Journal.*

Brown, P.M. 1997. Taxonomy and distribution of *Spiranthes casei* in northern New England. Master's thesis, University of Massachusetts–Dartmouth.

Case, F.W. 1987. *Orchids of the western Great Lakes region.* Rev. ed. Bulletin 48. Cranbrook Institute of Science, Bloomfield Hills, Mich.

Chapman, W.K. 1996. *Orchids of the Northeast: A field guide.* Syracuse University Press, Syracuse, N.Y.

Correll, D.S. 1978. *Native orchids of North America.* Stanford University Press, Stanford, Calif.

Keenan, P. 1986. *Field guide to the orchids of Maine.* DeLorme, Freeport, Maine.

Lamont, E.E. 1996. Atlas of the orchids of Long Island, N.Y. *Bulletin of the Torrey Botanical Club* 123(2):157–166.

Lamont, E.E., J.M. Beitel, and R.E. Zaremba. 1988. Current status of orchids on Long Island, New York. *Torreya* 115(2):113–121.

Latham, R.A. 1940. Distribution of wild orchids on Long Island. *Long Island Forum* 3:103–107.

Luer, C.A. 1975. *The native orchids of the United States and Canada, excluding Florida.* New York Botanical Garden, New York.

Petrie, W. 1981. *Guide to the orchids of North America.* Hancock House, Blaine, Wash.

Wallace, J. 1951. *The orchids of Maine.* University of Maine, Orono.

Whiting, R.E., and P.M. Catling. 1986. *Orchids of Ontario.* Canacoll Foundation, Ottawa, Canada.

Williams, J.G., and A.E. Williams. *Field guide to the orchids of North America.* Universe Books, New York.

The following references describe new taxa and new combinations. For the sake of brevity, I have not included titles of journal articles.

Amerorchis rotundifolia   **small round-leaved orchis**
  forma *immaculata*
Brown, P.M. 1995. *North American Native Orchid Journal* 1(2):132.
Johnson, L.P. 1995. *Lindleyana* 10(1):1.

Calopogon tuberosus   **grass-pink**
  (including var. *latifolius*)
Catling, P.M., and Z. Lucas. 1987. *Rhodora* 89:401–413.

Calypso bulbosa var. *americana*   **eastern fairy-slipper**
  forma *albiflora*
Brown, P.M. 1995. *North American Native Orchid Journal* 1(1):17.

Corallorhiza maculata var. *maculata*   **spotted coralroot**
Corallorhiza maculata var. *occidentalis*   **western spotted coralroot**
Brown, P.M. 1995. *North American Native Orchid Journal* 1(1):8; 1(3):197.
Case, F.W. 1987. *Orchids of the western Great Lakes region.* Cranbrook Institute of Science. Plate 42A,C.
Freudenstein, J.V. 1987. *Contributions from the University of Michigan Herbarium* 16:145–153.
Freudenstein, J.V. 1992. Ph.D. dissertation, Cornell University. P. 346.

Corallorhiza odontorhiza var. *pringlei*   **Pringle's autumn coralroot**
Case, F.W. 1987. *Orchids of the western Great Lakes region.* Cranbrook Institute of Science. Plate 43B.
Freudenstein, J.V. 1992. Ph.D. dissertation, Cornell University. P. 275.

Cypripedium acaule   **pink lady's-slipper, or moccasin flower**
  forma *biflorum*
Brown, P.M. 1995. *North American Native Orchid Journal* 1(3):201.

Cypripedium arietinum   **ram's-head lady's-slipper**
  forma *biflorum*
Brown, P.M. 1995. *North American Native Orchid Journal* 1(3):201.

Cypripedium parviflorum var. *parviflorum*   **southern small yellow lady's-slipper**
Cypripedium parviflorum var. *makasin*   **northern small yellow lady's-slipper**
Cypripedium parviflorum var. *pubescens*   **large yellow lady's-slipper**
Sheviak, C.J. 1992. *American Orchid Society Bulletin* 61(6):548; 1993, 62(4):403; 1994,
    63(6):664–669; 1995, 64(6):606–612.

Epipactis helleborine   **broad-leaved helleborine**
    forma *luteola*
Brown, P.M. 1996. *North American Native Orchid Journal* 2(4):316–318.

Goodyera oblongifolia   **giant rattlesnake orchid**
Eastman, L., R.L. Hinkle, and D.M. Dumond. 1982. *Rhodora* 84(838):311–313.

Goodyera repens forma *ophiodes*   **lesser rattlesnake orchis** (veined-leaf form)
Brown, P.M. 1995. *North American Native Orchid Journal* 1(1):14.

Listera auriculata   **auricled twayblade**
Platt, J.L., E. Yanuck-Platt, and C.J. Sheviak. 1982. *Rhodora* 84(840):547–549.

Listera australis   **southern twayblade**
    forma *trifolia*
Brown, P.M. 1995. *North American Native Orchid Journal* 1(1):11.

Listera convallarioides   **broad-lipped twayblade**
    forma *trifolia*
Brown, P.M. 1995. *North American Native Orchid Journal* 1(1):11.

Listera cordata var. *cordata*   **heart-leaved twayblade**
    forma *trifolia*, forma *variegata*
Brown, P.M. 1995. *North American Native Orchid Journal* 1(1):11.

Listera ×*veltmanii*   **Veltman's twayblade**
    (*L. auriculata* × *L. convallarioides*)
Case, F.W. 1964. *Michigan Botanist* 3:67–70.
Catling, P.M. 1976. *Rhodora* 78(814):261–269.

Malaxis bayardii   **Bayard's adder's-mouth**
Catling, P.M. 1991. *Lindleyana* 6:3-23.

Platanthera grandiflora   **large purple fringed orchis**
Stoutamire, W.P. 1974. *Brittonia* 26:42–58.
    forma *bicolor*, forma *carnea*
Brown, P.M. 1995. *North American Native Orchid Journal* 1(1):12.

Platanthera macrophylla   **Goldie's pad-leaved orchis, or large pad-leaved orchis**
Platanthera orbiculata   **pad-leaved orchis**
Ames, O. 1906. *Rhodora* 8:1–5.
Brown, P.M. 1988 (rev. 1992). *Wild Flower Notes* 3(1):23.
Reddoch, A.H., and J.M. Reddoch. 1993. *Lindleyana* 8(4):171–188.

Platanthera obtusata   **blunt-leaved rein orchis**
   forma *foliosa*
Brown, P.M. 1995. *North American Native Orchid Journal* 1(1):13.

Platanthera pallida   **pale fringed orchis**
Brown, P.M. 1992. *Novon* 2(4):308–311.

Platanthera psycodes   **small purple fringed orchis**
Stoutamire, W.P. 1974. *Brittonia* 26:42-58.
   forma *rosea*
Brown, P.M. 1995. *North American Native Orchid Journal* 1(3):201.

Patanthera ✕andrewsii   **Andrews' hybrid fringed orchis**
Platanthera ✕keenanii   **Keenan's hybrid fringed orchis**
Catling, P.M., and V.R. Catling. 1994. *Lindleyana* 9(1):19–32.

Spiranthes casei var. *casei*   **Case's ladies'-tresses**
Catling, P.M., and J.E. Cruise. 1974. *Rhodora* 76(808):256–536.

Spiranthes cernua   **nodding ladies'-tresses**
Sheviak, C.J. 1982. Bulletin 448. New York State Museum.
Sheviak, C.J. 1991. *Lindleyana* 6(4):228–234.

Spiranthes ochroleuca   **yellow ladies'-tresses**
Sheviak, C.J., and P.M. Catling. 1980. *Rhodora* 82(832):526–562.

Spiranthes ✕borealis   **northern hybrid ladies'-tresses**
Brown, P.M. 1995. *North American Native Orchid Journal* 1(4):290.

Spiranthes ✕intermedia   **intermediate hybrid ladies'-tresses**
   (*S. gracilis* ✕ *S. vernalis*)
Catling, P.M. 1978. *Rhodora* 80(823):377–389.

Spiranthes ✕simpsonii **Simpson's hybrid ladies'-tresses**
   (*Spiranthes lacera* var. *lacera* ✕ *S. romanzoffiana*)
Catling, P.M., and C.J. Sheviak. 1993. *Lindleyana* 8(2):77–81.
Simpson, R.C., and P.M. Catling. 1978. *Canadian Field Naturalist* 92(4):350–358.

Triphora trianthophora var. *trianthophora*   **three birds orchis, or nodding pogonia**
Williams, S.A. 1994. *Rhodora* 96(885):30–43.
   forma *albidoflava*
Keenan, P. 1992. *Rhodora* 94:38–39.

CHECKLIST OF THE ORCHIDS OF THE NORTHEAST

The following is a list of all the orchid species that have been found growing wild in the northeastern United States (New England, New York, and adjoining Pennsylvania and New Jersey). The species are listed in alphabetical order by genus and species, except in the case of hybrids, which are listed at the end of the relevant genus. An asterisk (*) indicates that the species is introduced. Following the checklist for the Northeast are checklists for individual states.

Amerorchis rotundifolia (Banks ex Pursh) Hultén
small round-leaved orchis

Aplectrum hyemale (Muhlenberg ex Willdenow) Torrey
putty-root, or Adam and Eve
    forma *pallidum* House: yellow-flowered form

Arethusa bulbosa Linnaeus
dragon's-mouth
    forma *albiflora* Rand & Redfield: white-flowered form
    forma *subcaerulea* Rand & Redfield: lilac blue–flowered form

Calopogon tuberosus (Linnaeus) Britton, Sterns & Poggenberg var. *tuberosus*
grass-pink
    forma *albiflorus* Britton: white-flowered form

Calypso bulbosa (Linnaeus) Oakes var. *americana* (R. Brown) Luer
eastern fairy-slipper
    forma *albiflora* P.M. Brown: white-flowered form

Coeloglossum viride (Linnaeus) Hartman var. *virescens* (Muhlenberg) Luer
long bracted green orchis

Corallorhiza maculata (Rafinesque) Rafinesque var. *maculata*
spotted coralroot
    forma *flavida* (C.H. Peck) Farwell: yellow-stemmed form
    forma *rubra* P.M. Brown: red-stemmed form
Corallorhiza maculata (Rafinesque) Rafinesque var. *occidentalis* (Lindley) Ames
western spotted coralroot
    forma *immaculata* (Peck) Howell: yellow spotless form

forma *intermedia* Farwell: brown-stemmed form
forma *punicea* (Bartlett) Weatherby & Adams: red-stemmed form

Corallorhiza odontorhiza (Willdenow) Nuttall var. *odontorhiza*
autumn coralroot
forma *flavida* Wherry: yellow-stemmed form
Corallorhiza odontorhiza (Willdenow) Nuttall var. *pringlei* (Greenman) Freudenstein, ined.
Pringle's autumn coralroot

Corallorhiza striata Lindley var. *striata*
striped coralroot

Corallorhiza trifida Chatelain
early coralroot

Cypripedium acaule Aiton
pink lady's-slipper, or moccasin flower
forma *albiflorum* Rand & Redfield: white-flowered form
forma *biflorum* P.M. Brown: two-flowered form

Cypripedium arietinum R. Brown
ram's-head lady's-slipper
forma *albiflorum* House: white-flowered form
forma *biflorum* P.M. Brown: two-flowered form

Cypripedium candidum Muhlenberg ex Willdenow
small white lady's-slipper

Cypripedium parviflorum Salisbury var. *parviflorum*
southern small yellow lady's-slipper
Cypripedium parviflorum Salisbury var. *makasin* (Farwell) Sheviak
northern small yellow lady's-slipper
Cypripedium parviflorum Salisbury var. *pubescens* (Willdenow) Knight
large yellow lady's-slipper

Cypripedium reginae Walter
showy lady's-slipper
forma *albolabium* Fernald & Schubert: white-flowered form

Cypripedium ×*andrewsii* Fuller nm. *andrewsii*
Andrews' hybrid lady's-slipper
(*C. candidum* × *C. parviflorum* var. *makasin*)

Cypripedium ×*andrewsii* Fuller nm. *favillianum* (Curtis) Boivin
Faville's hybrid lady's-slipper
(*C. candidum* × *C. parviflorum* var. *pubescens*)

Epipactis atrorubens (Berber) Besser
red helleborine*

Epipactis helleborine (Linnaeus) Cranz
broad-leaved helleborine*
    forma *alba* (Webster) Boivin: white-flowered form
    forma *luteola* P.M. Brown: yellow-flowered form
    forma *monotropoides* (Mousley) Scoggin: albino form
    forma *variegata* (Webster) Boivin: variegated form
    forma *viridens* A. Gray: green-flowered form

Galearis spectabilis (Linnaeus) Rafinesque
showy orchis
    forma *gordinierii* (House) Whiting & Catling: white-flowered form
    forma *willeyi* (Seymour) P.M. Brown: pink-flowered form

Goodyera oblongifolia Rafinesque
giant rattlesnake orchis
    forma *reticulata* (Boivin) P.M. Brown: reticulated-leaf form

Goodyera pubescens (Willdenow) R. Brown
downy rattlesnake orchis

Goodyera repens (Linnaeus) R. Brown forma *ophioides* (Fernald) P.M. Brown
lesser rattlesnake orchis: white-veined-leaf form

Goodyera tesselata Loddiges
checkered rattlesnake orchis

Gymnadenia conopsea (Linnaeus) R. Brown
fragrant orchis*

Isotria medeoloides (Pursh) Rafinesque
small whorled pogonia

Isotria verticillata (Willdenow) Rafinesque
large whorled pogonia

Liparis liliifolia (Linnaeus) Richard
lily-leaved twayblade
    forma *viridiflora* Wadmond: green-flowered form

Liparis loeselii (Linnaeus) Richard
Loesel's twayblade, or fen orchis

Listera auriculata Wiegand
auricled twayblade
    forma *trifolia* (Lepage) Lepage: three-leaved form

Listera australis Lindley
southern twayblade
    forma *trifolia* P.M. Brown: three-leaved form

Listera convallarioides (Swartz) Nuttall
broad-lipped twayblade
  forma *trifolia* P.M. Brown: three-leaved form

Listera cordata (Linnaeus) R. Brown var. *cordata*
heart-leaved twayblade
  forma *disjuncta* Lepage: alternate-leaved form
  forma *trifolia* P.M. Brown: three-leaved form
  forma *variegata* P.M. Brown: variegated-leaf form
  forma *viridens* P.M. Brown: green-flowered form

Listera smallii Wiegand
Small's twayblade

Listera ×*veltmanii* Case
Veltman's hybrid twayblade
  (*L. auriculata* × *L. convallarioides*)

Malaxis bayardii Fernald
Bayard's adder's-mouth

Malaxis brachypoda (Gray) Fernald
white adder's-mouth
  forma *bifolia* (Mousley) Fernald: two-leaved form

Malaxis unifolia Michaux
green adder's-mouth
  forma *bifolia* (Mousley) Fernald: two-leaved form

Platanthera blephariglottis (Willdenow) Lindley var. *blephariglottis*
northern white fringed orchis
  forma *holopetala* (Lindley) P.M. Brown: entire-lip form
Platanthera blephariglottis (Willdenow) Lindley var. *conspicua* (Ames) Luer
southern white fringed orchis

Platanthera ciliaris (Linnaeus) Lindley
orange (yellow) fringed orchis

Platanthera clavellata (Michaux) Luer var. *clavellata*
little club-spur orchis
Platanthera clavellata (Michaux) Luer var. *ophioglossoides* (Fernald) P.M. Brown
northern club-spur orchis

Platanthera cristata (Michaux) Lindley
orange (yellow) crested orchis

Platanthera dilatata (Pursh) Lindley var. *dilatata*
tall white northern bog orchis

Platanthera flava (Linnaeus) Lindley var. *herbiola* (R. Brown) Luer
northern tubercled orchis
   forma *lutea* (Boivin) Whiting & Catling: yellow-flowered form

Platanthera grandiflora (Bigelow) Lindley
large purple fringed orchis
   forma *albiflora* (Rand & Redfield) Catling: white-flowered form
   forma *carnea* P.M. Brown: pink-flowered form
   forma *mentotonsa* (Fernald) P.M. Brown: entire-lip form

Platanthera hookeri (Torrey) Lindley
Hooker's orchis

Platanthera huronensis (Linnaeus) Lindley
green bog orchis

Platanthera hyperborea (Linnaeus) Lindley var. *hyperborea*
northern green bog orchis

Platanthera lacera (Michaux) G. Don
green fringed orchis, or ragged orchis

Platanthera leucophaea (Nuttall) Lindley
eastern prairie fringed orchis

Platanthera macrophylla (Goldie) P.M. Brown
Goldie's pad-leaved orchis, or large pad-leaved orchis

Platanthera obtusata (Banks ex Pursh) Lindley
blunt-leaved rein orchis
   forma *foliosa* P.M. Brown: multiple-leaved form

Platanthera orbiculata (Pursh) Lindley
pad-leaved orchis

Platanthera pallida P.M. Brown
pale fringed orchis

Platanthera psycodes (Linnaeus) Lindley
small purple fringed orchis
   forma *albiflora* (R. Hoffman) Whiting & Catling: white-flowered form
   forma *ecalcarata* (Bryan) P.M. Brown: spurless form
   forma *rosea* P.M. Brown: pink-flowered form
   forma *varians* (Bryan) P.M. Brown: entire-lip form

Platanthera ×*andrewsii* (Niles) Luer
Andrews' hybrid fringed orchis
   (*P. lacera* × *P. psycodes*)

Platanthera ×*bicolor* (Rafinesque) Luer
bicolor hybrid fringed orchis
   (*P. blephariglottis* var. *conspicua* × *P. ciliaris*)

Platanthera ×*canbyi* (Ames) Luer
Canby's hybrid fringed orchis
   (*P. blephariglottis* var. *conspicua* × *P. cristata*)

Platanthera ×*channellii* Folsom
Channell's hybrid fringed orchis
   (*P. ciliaris* × *P. cristata*)

Platanthera ×*keenanii* P.M. Brown
Keenan's hybrid fringed orchis
   (*P. grandiflora* × *P. lacera*)

Platanthera ×*media* (Rydberg) Luer
intermediate hybrid rein orchis
   (*P. hyperborea* var. *hyperborea* × *P. dilatata* var. *dilatata*)

Platanthera ×*vossii* Case
Voss' hybrid rein orchis
   (*P. blephariglottis* var. *blephariglottis* × *P. clavellata* var. *ophioglossoides*)

Pogonia ophioglossoides (Linnaeus) Ker-Gawler var. *ophioglossoides*
rose pogonia
   forma *albiflora* Rand & Redfield: white-flowered form

Spiranthes casei Catling & Cruise var. *casei*
Case's ladies'-tresses

Spiranthes cernua (Linnaeus) L.C. Richard
nodding ladies'-tresses

Spiranthes lacera Rafinesque var. *lacera*
northern slender ladies'-tresses
Spiranthes lacera Rafinesque var. *gracilis* (Bigelow) Luer
southern slender ladies'-tresses

Spiranthes lucida (H.H. Eaton) Ames
shining ladies'-tresses

Spiranthes ochroleuca (Rydberg) Rydberg
yellow ladies'-tresses

Spiranthes praecox (Walter) S. Watson forma *albolabia* Brown & McCartney
giant ladies'-tresses: white-lipped form

Spiranthes romanzoffiana Chamisso
hooded ladies'-tresses

Spiranthes tuberosa Rafinesque
little ladies'-tresses

Spiranthes vernalis Engler & Gray
grass-leaved ladies'-tresses

Spiranthes ×*borealis* P.M. Brown
northern hybrid ladies'-tresses
  (*S. casei* × *S. ochroleuca*)

Spiranthes ×*intermedia* Ames
intermediate hybrid ladies'-tresses
  (*S. lacera* var. *gracilis* × *S. vernalis*)

Spiranthes ×*simpsonii* Catling & Sheviak
Simpson's hybrid ladies'-tresses
  (*S. lacera* var. *lacera* × *S. romanzoffiana*)

Tipularia discolor (Pursh) Nuttall
crane-fly orchis

Triphora trianthophora (Swartz) Rydberg var. *trianthophora*
three birds orchis, or nodding pogonia
  forma *albidoflava* Keenan: white-flowered form

Checklist for Maine

Amerorchis rotundifolia   **small round-leaved orchis**
Arethusa bulbosa   **dragon's-mouth**
Calopogon tuberosus var. *tuberosus*   **grass-pink**
Calypso bulbosa var. *americana*   **eastern fairy-slipper**
Coeloglossum viride var. *virescens*   **long bracted green orchis**
Corallorhiza maculata var. *maculata*   **spotted coralroot**
Corallorhiza maculata var. *occidentalis*   **western spotted coralroot**
Corallorhiza odontorhiza var. *odontorhiza*   **autumn coralroot**
Corallorhiza odontorhiza var. *pringlei*   **Pringle's autumn coralroot**
Corallorhiza trifida   **early coralroot**
Cypripedium acaule   **pink lady's-slipper, or moccasin flower**
Cypripedium arietinum   **ram's-head lady's-slipper**
Cypripedium parviflorum var. *makasin*   **northern small yellow lady's-slipper**
Cypripedium parviflorum var. *pubescens*   **large yellow lady's-slipper**
Cypripedium reginae   **showy lady's-slipper**
Epipactis helleborine   **broad-leaved helleborine***

Galearis spectabilis   **showy orchis**
Goodyera oblongifolia   **giant rattlesnake orchis**
Goodyera pubescens   **downy rattlesnake orchis**
Goodyera repens   **lesser rattlesnake orchis**
Goodyera tesselata   **checkered rattlesnake orchis**
Isotria medeoloides   **small whorled pogonia**
Isotria verticillata   **large whorled pogonia**
Liparis loeselii   **Loesel's twayblade, or fen orchis**
Listera auriculata   **auricled twayblade**
Listera convallarioides   **broad-lipped twayblade**
Listera cordata var. *cordata*   **heart-leaved twayblade**
Malaxis brachypoda   **white adder's-mouth**
Malaxis unifolia   **green adder's-mouth**
Platanthera blephariglottis var. *blephariglottis*   **white fringed orchis**
Platanthera clavellata var. *clavellata*   **little club-spur orchis**
Platanthera clavellata var. *ophioglossoides*   **northern club-spur orchis**
Platanthera dilatata var. *dilatata*   **tall white northern bog orchis**
Platanthera flava var. *herbiola*   **northern tubercled orchis**
Platanthera grandiflora   **large purple fringed orchis**
Platanthera hookeri   **Hooker's orchis**
Platanthera huronensis   **green bog orchis**
Platanthera hyperborea var. *hyperborea*   **northern green bog orchis**
Platanthera lacera   **green fringed orchis, or ragged orchis**
Platanthera leucophaea   **eastern prairie fringed orchis**
Platanthera macrophylla   **Goldie's pad-leaved orchis, or large pad-leaved orchis**
Platanthera obtusata   **blunt-leaved rein orchis**
Platanthera orbiculata   **pad-leaved orchis**
Platanthera psycodes   **small purple fringed orchis**
Pogonia ophioglossoides var. *ophioglossoides*   **rose pogonia**
Spiranthes casei var. *casei*   **Case's ladies'-tresses**
Spiranthes cernua   **nodding ladies'-tresses**
Spiranthes lacera var. *lacera*   **northern slender ladies'-tresses**
Spiranthes lacera var. *gracilis*   **southern slender ladies'-tresses**
Spiranthes lucida   **shining ladies'-tresses**
Spiranthes ochroleuca   **yellow ladies'-tresses**
Spiranthes romanzoffiana   **hooded ladies'-tresses**
Triphora trianthophora var. *trianthophora*   **three birds orchis, or nodding pogonia**

Checklist for New Hampshire

Arethusa bulbosa   **dragon's-mouth**
Calopogon tuberosus var. *tuberosus*   **grass-pink**
Calypso bulbosa var. *americana*   **eastern fairy-slipper**
Coeloglossum viride var. *virescens*   **long bracted green orchis**

Corallorhiza maculata var. *maculata*   **spotted coralroot**
Corallorhiza maculata var. *occidentalis*   **western spotted coralroot**
Corallorhiza odontorhiza var. *odontorhiza*   **autumn coralroot**
Corallorhiza trifida   **early coralroot**
Cypripedium acaule   **pink lady's-slipper, or moccasin flower**
Cypripedium arietinum   **ram's-head lady's-slipper**
Cypripedium parviflorum var. *makasin*   **northern small yellow lady's-slipper**
Cypripedium parviflorum var. *pubescens*   **large yellow lady's-slipper**
Cypripedium reginae   **showy lady's-slipper**
Epipactis helleborine   **broad-leaved helleborine***
Galearis spectabilis   **showy orchis**
Goodyera pubescens   **downy rattlesnake orchis**
Goodyera repens   **lesser rattlesnake orchis**
Goodyera tesselata   **checkered rattlesnake orchis**
Isotria medeoloides   **small whorled pogonia**
Isotria verticillata   **large whorled pogonia**
Liparis loeselii   **Loesel's twayblade, or fen orchis**
Listera auriculata   **auricled twayblade**
Listera convallarioides   **broad-lipped twayblade**
Listera cordata var. *cordata*   **heart-leaved twayblade**
Malaxis brachypoda   **white adder's-mouth**
Malaxis unifolia   **green adder's-mouth**
Platanthera blephariglottis var. *blephariglottis*   **northern white fringed orchis**
Platanthera clavellata var. *clavellata*   **little club-spur orchis**
Platanthera clavellata var. *ophioglossoides*   **northern club-spur orchis**
Platanthera dilatata var. *dilatata*   **tall white northern bog orchis**
Platanthera flava var. *herbiola*   **northern tubercled orchis**
Platanthera grandiflora   **large purple fringed orchis**
Platanthera hookeri   **Hooker's orchis**
Platanthera huronensis   **green bog orchis**
Platanthera hyperborea var. *hyperborea*   **northern green bog orchis**
Platanthera lacera   **green fringed orchis, or ragged orchis**
Platanthera macrophylla   **Goldie's pad-leaved orchis, or large pad-leaved orchis**
Platanthera obtusata   **blunt-leaved rein orchis**
Platanthera orbiculata   **pad-leaved orchis**
Platanthera psycodes   **small purple fringed orchis**
Pogonia ophioglossoides var. *ophioglossoides*   **rose pogonia**
Spiranthes casei var. *casei*   **Case's ladies'-tresses**
Spiranthes cernua   **nodding ladies'-tresses**
Spiranthes lacera var. *lacera*   **northern slender ladies'-tresses**
Spiranthes lacera var. *gracilis*   **southern slender ladies'-tresses**
Spiranthes lucida   **shining ladies'-tresses**
Spiranthes ochroleuca   **yellow ladies'-tresses**
Spiranthes romanzoffiana   **hooded ladies'-tresses**
Spiranthes vernalis   **grass-leaved ladies'-tresses**
Triphora trianthophora var. *trianthophora*   **three birds orchis, or nodding pogonia**

Checklist for Vermont

Amerorchis rotundifolia   **small round-leaved orchis**
Aplectrum hyemale   **putty-root, or Adam and Eve**
Arethusa bulbosa   **dragon's-mouth**
Calopogon tuberosus var. *tuberosus*   **grass-pink**
Calypso bulbosa var. *americana*   **eastern fairy-slipper**
Coeloglossum viride var. *virescens*   **long bracted green orchis**
Corallorhiza maculata var. *maculata*   **spotted coralroot**
Corallorhiza maculata var. *occidentalis*   **western spotted coralroot**
Corallorhiza odontorhiza var. *odontorhiza*   **autumn coralroot**
Corallorhiza odontorhiza var. *pringlei*   **Pringle's autumn coralroot**
Corallorhiza trifida   **early coralroot**
Cypripedium acaule   **pink lady's-slipper, or moccasin flower**
Cypripedium arietinum   **ram's-head lady's-slipper**
Cypripedium parviflorum var. *makasin*   **northern small yellow lady's-slipper**
Cypripedium parviflorum var. *pubescens*   **large yellow lady's-slipper**
Cypripedium reginae   **showy lady's-slipper**
Epipactis atrorubens   **red helleborine***
Epipactis helleborine   **broad-leaved helleborine***
Galearis spectabilis   **showy orchis**
Goodyera pubescens   **downy rattlesnake orchis**
Goodyera repens   **lesser rattlesnake orchis**
Goodyera tesselata   **checkered rattlesnake orchis**
Isotria medeoloides   **small whorled pogonia**
Isotria verticillata   **large whorled pogonia**
Liparis liliifolia   **lily-leaved twayblade**
Liparis loeselii   **Loesel's twayblade, or fen orchis**
Listera auriculata   **auricled twayblade**
Listera australis   **southern twayblade**
Listera convallarioides   **broad-lipped twayblade**
Listera cordata var. *cordata*   **heart-leaved twayblade**
Malaxis brachypoda   **white adder's-mouth**
Malaxis unifolia   **green adder's-mouth**
Platanthera blephariglottis var. *blephariglottis*   **white fringed orchis**
Platanthera clavellata var. *ophioglossoides*   **northern club-spur orchis**
Platanthera dilatata var. *dilatata*   **tall white northern bog orchis**
Platanthera flava var. *herbiola*   **northern tubercled orchis**
Platanthera grandiflora   **large purple fringed orchis**
Platanthera hookeri   **Hooker's orchis**
Platanthera huronensis   **green bog orchis**
Platanthera hyperborea var. *hyperborea*   **northern green bog orchis**
Platanthera lacera   **green fringed orchis, or ragged orchis**
Platanthera macrophylla   **Goldie's pad-leaved orchis, or large pad-leaved orchis**
Platanthera obtusata   **blunt-leaved rein orchis**
Platanthera orbiculata   **pad-leaved orchis**
Platanthera psycodes   **small purple fringed orchis**

Pogonia ophioglossoides var. *ophioglossoides*   **rose pogonia**
Spiranthes casei var. *casei*   **Case's ladies'-tresses**
Spiranthes cernua   **nodding ladies'-tresses**
Spiranthes lacera var. *lacera*   **northern slender ladies'-tresses**
Spiranthes lacera var. *gracilis*   **southern slender ladies'-tresses**
Spiranthes lucida   **shining ladies'-tresses**
Spiranthes ochroleuca   **yellow ladies'-tresses**
Spiranthes romanzoffiana   **hooded ladies'-tresses**
Triphora trianthophora var. *trianthophora*   **three birds orchis, or nodding pogonia**

Checklist for Massachusetts

Aplectrum hyemale   **putty-root, or Adam and Eve**
Arethusa bulbosa   **dragon's-mouth**
Calopogon tuberosus var. *tuberosus*   **grass-pink**
Coeloglossum viride var. *virescens*   **long bracted green orchis**
Corallorhiza maculata var. *maculata*   **spotted coralroot**
Corallorhiza maculata var. *occidentalis*   **western spotted coralroot**
Corallorhiza odontorhiza var. *odontorhiza*   **autumn coralroot**
Corallorhiza odontorhiza var. *pringlei*   **Pringle's autumn coralroot**
Corallorhiza trifida   **early coralroot**
Cypripedium acaule   **pink lady's-slipper, or moccasin flower**
Cypripedium arietinum   **ram's-head lady's-slipper**
Cypripedium parviflorum var. *parviflorum*   **southern small yellow lady's-slipper**
Cypripedium parviflorum var. *makasin*   **northern small yellow lady's-slipper**
Cypripedium parviflorum var. *pubescens*   **large yellow lady's-slipper**
Cypripedium reginae   **showy lady's-slipper**
Epipactis helleborine   **broad-leaved helleborine***
Galearis spectabilis   **showy orchis**
Goodyera pubescens   **downy rattlesnake orchis**
Goodyera repens   **lesser rattlesnake orchis**
Goodyera tesselata   **checkered rattlesnake orchis**
Isotria medeoloides   **small whorled pogonia**
Isotria verticillata   **large whorled pogonia**
Liparis liliifolia   **lily-leaved twayblade**
Liparis loeselii   **Loesel's twayblade, or fen orchis**
Listera cordata var. *cordata*   **heart-leaved twayblade**
Malaxis bayardii   **Bayard's adder's-mouth**
Malaxis brachypoda   **white adder's-mouth**
Malaxis unifolia   **green adder's-mouth**
Platanthera blephariglottis var. *blephariglottis*   **northern white fringed orchis**
Platanthera blephariglottis var. *conspicua*   **southern white fringed orchis**
Platanthera ciliaris   **orange (yellow) fringed orchis**
Platanthera clavellata var. *clavellata*   **little club-spur orchis**
Platanthera clavellata var. *ophioglossoides*   **northern club-spur orchis**
Platanthera cristata   **orange (yellow) crested orchis**

Platanthera dilatata var. *dilatata*   **tall white northern bog orchis**
Platanthera flava var. *herbiola*   **northern tubercled orchis**
Platanthera grandiflora   **large purple fringed orchis**
Platanthera hookeri   **Hooker's orchis**
Platanthera huronensis   **green bog orchis**
Platanthera hyperborea var. *hyperborea*   **northern green bog orchis**
Platanthera lacera   **green fringed orchis, or ragged orchis**
Platanthera macrophylla   **Goldie's pad-leaved orchis, or large pad-leaved orchis**
Platanthera obtusata   **blunt-leaved rein orchis**
Platanthera orbiculata   **pad-leaved orchis**
Platanthera psycodes   **small purple fringed orchis**
Pogonia ophioglossoides var. *ophioglossoides*   **rose pogonia**
Spiranthes cernua   **nodding ladies'-tresses**
Spiranthes lacera var. *lacera*   **northern slender ladies'-tresses**
Spiranthes lacera var. *gracilis*   **southern slender ladies'-tresses**
Spiranthes lucida   **shining ladies'-tresses**
Spiranthes ochroleuca   **yellow ladies'-tresses**
Spiranthes romanzoffiana   **hooded ladies'-tresses**
Spiranthes tuberosa   **little ladies'-tresses**
Spiranthes vernalis   **grass-leaved ladies'-tresses**
Tipularia discolor   **crane-fly orchis**
Triphora trianthophora var. *trianthophora*   **three birds orchis, or nodding pogonia**

Checklist for Rhode Island

Arethusa bulbosa   **dragon's-mouth**
Calopogon tuberosus var. *tuberosus*   **grass-pink**
Coeloglossum viride var. *virescens*   **long bracted green orchis**
Corallorhiza maculata var. *maculata*   **spotted coralroot**
Corallorhiza odontorhiza var. *odontorhiza*   **autumn coralroot**
Corallorhiza trifida   **early coralroot**
Cypripedium acaule   **pink lady's-slipper, or moccasin flower**
Cypripedium parviflorum var. *parviflorum*   **southern small yellow lady's-slipper**
Cypripedium parviflorum var. *pubescens*   **large yellow lady's-slipper**
Epipactis helleborine   **broad-leaved helleborine***
Galearis spectabilis   **showy orchis**
Goodyera pubescens   **downy rattlesnake orchis**
Goodyera tesselata   **checkered rattlesnake orchis**
Isotria medeoloides   **small whorled pogonia**
Isotria verticillata   **large whorled pogonia**
Liparis liliifolia   **lily-leaved twayblade**
Liparis loeselii   **Loesel's twayblade, or fen orchis**
Listera cordata var. *cordata*   **heart-leaved twayblade**
Malaxis bayardii   **Bayard's adder's-mouth**
Malaxis brachypoda   **white adder's-mouth**
Malaxis unifolia   **green adder's-mouth**

Platanthera blephariglottis var. *blephariglottis*   **northern white fringed orchis**
Platanthera blephariglottis var. *conspicua*   **southern white fringed orchis**
Platanthera ciliaris   **orange (yellow) fringed orchis**
Platanthera clavellata var. *clavellata*   **little club-spur orchis**
Platanthera clavellata var. *ophioglossoides*   **northern club-spur orchis**
Platanthera flava var. *herbiola*   **northern tubercled orchis**
Platanthera grandiflora   **large purple fringed orchis**
Platanthera hookeri   **Hooker's orchis**
Platanthera lacera   **green fringed orchis, or ragged orchis**
Platanthera macrophylla   **Goldie's pad-leaved orchis, or large pad-leaved orchis**
Platanthera orbiculata   **pad-leaved orchis**
Platanthera psycodes   **small purple fringed orchis**
Pogonia ophioglossoides var. *ophioglossoides*   **rose pogonia**
Spiranthes cernua   **nodding ladies'-tresses**
Spiranthes lacera var. *gracilis*   **southern slender ladies'-tresses**
Spiranthes lucida   **shining ladies'-tresses**
Spiranthes ochroleuca   **yellow ladies'-tresses**
Spiranthes tuberosa   **little ladies'-tresses**
Spiranthes vernalis   **grass-leaved ladies'-tresses**

Checklist for Connecticut

Aplectrum hyemale   **putty-root, or Adam and Eve**
Arethusa bulbosa   **dragon's-mouth**
Calopogon tuberosus var. *tuberosus*   **grass-pink**
Coeloglossum viride var. *virescens*   **long bracted green orchis**
Corallorhiza maculata var. *maculata*   **spotted coralroot**
Corallorhiza odontorhiza var. *odontorhiza*   **autumn coralroot**
Corallorhiza odontorhiza var. *pringlei*   **Pringle's autumn coralroot**
Corallorhiza trifida   **early coralroot**
Cypripedium acaule   **pink lady's-slipper, or moccasin flower**
Cypripedium arietinum   **ram's-head lady's-slipper**
Cypripedium parviflorum var. *parviflorum*   **southern small yellow lady's-slipper**
Cypripedium parviflorum var. *makasin*   **northern small yellow lady's-slipper**
Cypripedium parviflorum var. *pubescens*   **large yellow lady's-slipper**
Cypripedium reginae   **showy lady's-slipper**
Epipactis helleborine   **broad-leaved helleborine***
Galearis spectabilis   **showy orchis**
Goodyera pubescens   **downy rattlesnake orchis**
Goodyera repens   **lesser rattlesnake orchis**
Goodyera tesselata   **checkered rattlesnake orchis**
Gymnadenia conopsea   **fragrant orchis***
Isotria medeoloides   **small whorled pogonia**
Isotria verticillata   **large whorled pogonia**
Liparis liliifolia   **lily-leaved twayblade**
Liparis loeselii   **Loesel's twayblade, or fen orchis**

Listera cordata var. *cordata*   heart-leaved twayblade
Malaxis bayardii   Bayard's adder's-mouth
Malaxis brachypoda   white adder's-mouth
Malaxis unifolia   green adder's-mouth
Platanthera blephariglottis var. *blephariglottis*   northern white fringed orchis
Platanthera blephariglottis var. *conspicua*   southern white fringed orchis
Platanthera ciliaris   orange (yellow) fringed orchis
Platanthera clavellata var. *clavellata*   little club-spur orchis
Platanthera clavellata var. *ophioglossoides*   northern club-spur orchis
Platanthera dilatata var. *dilatata*   tall white northern bog orchis
Platanthera flava var. *herbiola*   northern tubercled orchis
Platanthera grandiflora   large purple fringed orchis
Platanthera hookeri   Hooker's orchis
Platanthera huronensis   green bog orchis
Platanthera lacera   green fringed orchis, or ragged orchis
Platanthera macrophylla   Goldie's pad-leaved orchis, or large pad-leaved orchis
Platanthera orbiculata   pad-leaved orchis
Platanthera psycodes   small purple fringed orchis
Pogonia ophioglossoides var. *ophioglossoides*   rose pogonia
Spiranthes cernua   nodding ladies'-tresses
Spiranthes lacera var. *lacera*   northern slender ladies'-tresses
Spiranthes lacera var. *gracilis*   southern slender ladies'-tresses
Spiranthes lucida   shining ladies'-tresses
Spiranthes ochroleuca   yellow ladies'-tresses
Spiranthes tuberosa   little ladies'-tresses
Spiranthes vernalis   grass-leaved ladies'-tresses
Triphora trianthophora var. *trianthophora*   three birds orchis, or nodding pogonia

Checklist for New York

Amerorchis rotundifolia   small round-leaved orchis
Aplectrum hyemale   putty-root, or Adam and Eve
Arethusa bulbosa   dragon's-mouth
Calopogon tuberosus var. *tuberosus*   grass-pink
Calypso bulbosa var. *americana*   eastern fairy-slipper
Coeloglossum viride var. *virescens*   long bracted green orchis
Corallorhiza maculata var. *maculata*   spotted coralroot
Corallorhiza maculata var. *occidentalis*   western spotted coralroot
Corallorhiza odontorhiza var. *odontorhiza*   autumn coralroot
Corallorhiza odontorhiza var. *pringlei*   Pringle's autumn coralroot
Corallorhiza striata var. *striata*   striped coralroot
Corallorhiza trifida   early coralroot
Cypripedium acaule   pink lady's-slipper, or moccasin flower
Cypripedium arietinum   ram's-head lady's-slipper
Cypripedium candidum   small white lady's-slipper

Cypripedium parviflorum var. *parviflorum*   **southern small yellow lady's-slipper**
Cypripedium parviflorum var. *makasin*   **northern small yellow lady's-slipper**
Cypripedium parviflorum var. *pubescens*   **large yellow lady's-slipper**
Cypripedium reginae   **showy lady's-slipper**
Epipactis helleborine   **broad-leaved helleborine***
Galearis spectabilis   **showy orchis**
Goodyera pubescens   **downy rattlesnake orchis**
Goodyera repens   **lesser rattlesnake orchis**
Goodyera tesselata   **checkered rattlesnake orchis**
Isotria medeoloides   **small whorled pogonia**
Isotria verticillata   **large whorled pogonia**
Liparis liliifolia   **lily-leaved twayblade**
Liparis loeselii   **Loesel's twayblade, or fen orchis**
Listera auriculata   **auricled twayblade**
Listera australis   **southern twayblade**
Listera convallarioides   **broad-lipped twayblade**
Listera cordata var. *cordata*   **heart-leaved twayblade**
Malaxis bayardii   **Bayard's adder's-mouth**
Malaxis brachypoda   **white adder's-mouth**
Malaxis unifolia   **green adder's-mouth**
Platanthera blephariglottis var. *blephariglottis*   **northern white fringed orchis**
Platanthera blephariglottis var. *conspicua*   **southern white fringed orchis**
Platanthera ciliaris   **orange (yellow) fringed orchis**
Platanthera clavellata var. *clavellata*   **little club-spur orchis**
Platanthera clavellata var. *ophioglossoides*   **northern club-spur orchis**
Platanthera cristata   **orange (yellow) crested orchis**
Platanthera dilatata var. *dilatata*   **tall white northern bog orchis**
Platanthera flava var. *herbiola*   **northern tubercled orchis**
Platanthera grandiflora   **large purple fringed orchis**
Platanthera hookeri   **Hooker's orchis**
Platanthera huronensis   **green bog orchis**
Platanthera hyperborea var. *hyperborea*   **northern green bog orchis**
Platanthera lacera   **green fringed orchis, or ragged orchis**
Platanthera leucophaea   **eastern prairie fringed orchis**
Platanthera macrophylla   **Goldie's pad-leaved orchis, or large pad-leaved orchis**
Platanthera obtusata   **blunt-leaved rein orchis**
Platanthera orbiculata   **pad-leaved orchis**
Platanthera pallida   **pale fringed orchis**
Platanthera psycodes   **small purple fringed orchis**
Pogonia ophioglossoides var. *ophioglossoides*   **rose pogonia**
Spiranthes casei var. *casei*   **Case's ladies'-tresses**
Spiranthes cernua   **nodding ladies'-tresses**
Spiranthes lacera var. *lacera*   **northern slender ladies'-tresses**
Spiranthes lacera var. *gracilis*   **southern slender ladies'-tresses**
Spiranthes lucida   **shining ladies'-tresses**
Spiranthes ochroleuca   **yellow ladies'-tresses**
Spiranthes praecox   **giant ladies'-tresses**

Spiranthes romanzoffiana   **hooded ladies'-tresses**
Spiranthes tuberosa   **little ladies'-tresses**
Spiranthes vernalis   **grass-leaved ladies'-tresses**
Tipularia discolor   **crane-fly orchis**
Triphora trianthophora var. *trianthophora*   **three birds orchis, or nodding pogonia**

GLOSSARY

albino an individual lacking all color; example: *Epipactis helleborine* forma *monotropoides*; term often misapplied to white-flowered forms of otherwise colored flowers; example: *Cypripedium reginae* forma *albolabium*

auricle an appendage at the base of the lip; example: *Listera auriculata*

axillary occurring within the leaves

basal at or near the ground; example: leaves of *Platanthera hookeri*

bract, floral a reduced leaflike structure often at the base of a flower; example: *Coeloglossum viride* var. *virescens* (syn. *Habenaria viridis* var. *bracteata*)

bract, stem a reduced leaflike structure on the stem approaching the inflorescence or on a scape; example: many *Spiranthes* species

calcareous soil with a high pH, usually resulting from the presence of calcium; examples: limestone, marble

cauline attached to the stem above the ground; example: leaves of *Cypripedium parviflorum*

chasmogamous fertilized when flower parts are open, or fully expanded; example: *Corallorhiza odontorhiza* var. *pringlei*

cleistogamous fertilized within the bud, or when the flower parts are not expanded; example: *Corallorhiza odontorhiza* var. *odontorhiza*

cordate heart shaped; example: leaves of *Listera cordata* var. *cordata*

dilated widened or expanded; example: lip of *Platanthera dilatata*

fringed with the petals or sepals divided into small segments

inflorescence the flowering portion of the plant

lateral at the side; attached to the side

lip one of the three petals of an orchid, usually different in shape from the other two

mesic moderately moist; term often applied to sugar maple–beech forests growing in basic soils

nm. nothomorph; the taxonomic designation used for a hybrid that results from the interspecific crossing of two varieties or a variety and a species; example: *Cypripedium* ×*andrewsii* nm. *favillianum* is the result of the cross between *C. candidum* and *C. parviflorum* var. *pubescens*

ovary the portion of the flower at the very base of the perianth where the seed is developed

panduriform   fiddle-shaped; example: the lip of *Spiranthes romanzoffiana*

pedicel   the stem or stalk of an individual flower

perianth   a collective term for the petals and sepals

petal   one of the three inner parts of the perianth; in orchids this term describes the two lateral petals, which are differentiated from the lip, the third petal

pubescent   covered with soft, downy hairs; example: *Goodyera pubescens* plant

reticulate   with a distinct network of netted veins; example: leaves of *Goodyera oblongifolia* forma *reticulata*

scape   a leafless flower stem; example: *Cypripedium acaule*

sepal   one of the three outer parts of the perianth; in orchids the sepals are often the same color as the petals, but in the genus *Cypripedium* the sepals take on a different shape, and two may be joined and appear as one; example: *Cypripedium parviflorum*

serpentine   a geological formation that is usually very high in toxic metals such as nickel and magnesium; the rock is often green and has a slippery surface because of the talc or asbestos it contains; although serpentines support very few orchid species, these tend to be of special interest

spatulate   with the shape of a spatula, oblong and broadened at one end; example: petals of *Platanthera grandiflora*

spur   an extension of the lip that often contains nectar; example: flower of *Platanthera macrophylla*

station   a specific site of a plant or colony in the wild

tepal   a collective term for the petals and sepals, especially when they have the same appearance

terminal   term usually applied to a single flower or cluster of flowers at the summit of a stem or scape; examples: *Calypso bulbosa*, *Platanthera grandiflora*

thrifty   growing in abundance

throat   the upper portion of the lip in a species in which the lip is constricted

tubercle   a small projection; example: the projection on the lip of *Platanthera flava* var. *herbiola*

voucher   to collect, document, and dry and mount a plant from a specific site

whorl   three or more leaves attached at the same point; example: *Isotria verticillata*

PHOTO CREDITS

With a few exceptions the color photographs in this book were taken by the author. The vast majority were shot within New England and New York, but it was occasionally necessary to include specimens photographed elsewhere.

The following persons graciously loaned photographs to supplement those of the author:

Roger Bradley: *Corallorhiza odontorhiza* var. *odontorhiza* forma *flavida*, *Epipactis helleborine* forma *monotropoides*
Shirley A. Curtis: *Cypripedium arietinum* forma *albiflorum*
Dennis Horn: *Aplectrum hyemale* forma *pallidum*
Philip E. Keenan: *Triphora trianthophora* var. *trianthophora* forma *albido-flava*
Dick Sooy: *Platanthera* ×*vossii*

INDEX

Page numbers in **boldface** indicate the main text descriptions. Those in *italics* indicate locations in the keys. Color photos 1–64 follow page 84, color photos 65–128 follow page 196, and color photos 129–192 follow page 204.